Farmer's Daughters

Memories of Life on a Dairy Farm

Sharon Burns Ward and Teresa Burns Callahan

Farmer's Daughters: Memories of Life on a Dairy Farm © 2025 Sharon Burns Ward and Teresa Burns Callahan

First Stillwater River Publications Edition

ISBN: 978-1-968548-41-4
12345678910
Written by Sharon Burns Ward and Teresa Burns Callahan.
Published by Stillwater River Publications, West Warwick, RI, USA.

Acknowledgements

Thank you to our siblings, Donna and Tom, for all the great memories.

We dedicate this book:

To our parents,
Tom and Janet Burns,
whose support, guidance, and unconditional love
have been the foundation of our endeavors and
the inspiration behind this work.

"Tell it to your children,
And let your children tell it to their children,
and their children to the next generation."
- Joel 1:3

Contents

INTRODUCTION

Growing up on a farm has been one of life's greatest blessings. We wouldn't trade it for the world. We did not get the chance to travel or go on vacation as kids, but we had so much more available to us than most people. Our backyard was over 170 acres, which was our playground. We have a story at each and every nook of that farm. It's been our goal for a long time to put these memories to paper. Remembering these stories has been bittersweet but has brought us much joy and laughter in the process.

We were fortunate to live in a time when small family farms were the norm. Over the last five decades we have seen the demise of our family farms as the majority of our food is now produced by large agricultural corporations, "Big Ag." It is all too common now to see empty, dilapidated barns where there were once thriving working farms. Homes are now accented with reclaimed barn wood sourced from across the country, a rustic reminder of what used to be.

St. Mary's Church, Little Falls

In the beginning......

Our parents met on a blind date that was arranged by their parish priest, Fr. Halloran. Dad had taken her to a hockey game, which was not exactly Mom's cup of tea, but she gave him another chance and their romance blossomed. Janet T. Walker married Thomas J. Burns on August 12, 1961. Mom grew up in the city of Little Falls, while Dad lived on his family's dairy farm just a few miles away. After they bought the old O'Hara Farm on Middleville Road, life would be very different for her from that point on. She had become a farmer's wife.

Mom & Dad before they married

Married August 12, 1961

1973

SECTION ONE

FARM LIFE

The Farmer

Our Dad, Tom, AKA "Burnsy," is a farmer, teacher, preacher, and lover of all things related to the weather and farming. He is a fourth-generation dairy farmer and bought his own farm on Middleville Road in Little Falls, New York, shortly after he married our mom. This is where they raised the four of us kids until he could no longer afford to keep the farm going. Dad sold our farm around the time we went off to college. Mom and Dad eventually moved back into Dad's childhood farm on Cole Road where they live today. He learned how to grow the sweetest ear of corn around; Burns Sweet Corn has been legendary in Little Falls for over fifty years.

One of Dad's many talents is connecting with people through his warm personality and gift of gab. Everyone who meets him learns immediately that he is a genuine and honest man; salt of the earth. He will talk with anybody and is truly interested in hearing their story. Anyone that drives by the farm will usually see him waving hello with his hand high in the air.

Dad is also known to share his secrets to good health: cayenne pepper, apple cider vinegar, manuka honey, and a clove of garlic could cure all of your ailments.

Along with farming, he became a top oil salesman for Cen-pe-co (Central Petroleum Company) earning numerous awards for salesman of the year.

Dad's bachelor days

Dad is a wise and faithful man who has strong beliefs and isn't afraid to talk politics or religion. He tells us that whenever adversity comes our way, we just need to "rise to the occasion" and "take the high road." Over the years he has taught us and dozens of hired hands the importance of a hard day's work. One of his key life lessons is "attitude is everything." We hope that one day our children's children will appreciate Burnsy's wisdom and that they too will rise to the occasion.

1

Early days on the farm 1973

Dad showing off his cow

Dad's typical wave while baling hay

Dad's contagious laugh

Dad 2014

Evening silhouette

The Farmer's Wife

Our mom, Janet, AKA "Jansy" or "Gooch," is modest, humble, and was steadfast in her role as a farmer's wife. She rarely complained. She never took a day off or spent time doing something special for herself. She was always there for us and we always felt loved and supported. There was always dinner in the oven and laundry in the washer. Being a mother now, we wonder how she handled the endless chores, loads of smelly barn clothes, and the mud traipsed across the kitchen floor.

We didn't have much money but Mom was frugal enough to keep us well cared for. We had a big garden that Mom tended to. We also had a freezer full of meat from the bull we butchered every year. Of course, we had our own fresh milk that we brought up from the milk house in a jug every day. We also had endless sweet corn in the summer. As kids, little did we know that these things were sustaining our family.

Mom loved the animals, taking care of the cats and dogs that we had brought into the house. She also loved flowers and plants and managed to take time to care for her flower beds. She spent a lot of time with her mother "Gram Bam" as we called her, who came up frequently to help out. Mom had a gentle way of guiding us along. She would give us a stern look at times when we needed it, but we don't think she ever used that wooden paddle she kept on the chair in the kitchen. She had a strong but quiet faith and made sure we attended church every Sunday in our best clothes. She must have nearly died from worry watching us around those big animals and farm equipment, but if she was nervous, we didn't notice.

Mom became a teacher's aide at BOCES after we left our Middleville Road farm. She loved helping children with disabilities. She also enjoyed being a Eucharistic minister at our church, bringing communion to the hospitalized and homebound. She is sweet and humble, loved by all, and she never had an unkind word for others. She always put our needs first. We are forever grateful for her strength and selflessness.

1963 - Mom with Donna

1965 - Donna, Tom and baby Sharon

Mom on a typical day

Mom on her birthday

Tending to her plants 2015

Headed to her class reunion

Mom's beautiful smile 2016

The Farm Kids

There are four of us Burns kids: Donna (the eldest), Tommy, Sharon, and Teresa, (the youngest). We were all born between 1962 and 1968; four kids in just six years. Mom must have been exhausted taking care of us—Dad was probably thrilled to have the extra helping hands on the farm.

Us two youngest sisters were three years apart and shared a bedroom. Tommy and Donna had their own rooms, which we were envious of, but we learned how to share our space and our clothes early on. We created an imaginary line dividing our sides of the room. We enjoyed changing up the layout of our room from time to time to freshen it up. Our tiny corner closet was stuffed to the gills, and most of our clothes ended up in piles across the floor. We would often get frustrated when we

Donna, Teresa, Sharon and Tom 1969

Cooling off

School picture day 1974

Formal portrait of the four kids

Visit to Grandma's house-1972

couldn't find something and would yell down "Mom, where are my jeans?!" when they were likely buried at the bottom of a pile.

Our bedroom walls were covered with pink and yellow floral wallpaper, our bedspreads were pink with ruffled trim, and we painted our dressers bubblegum pink to match. Over the years our decor consisted of various posters of our favorite horses and pop stars like Sean Cassidy, Rick Springfield, and Andy Gibb. Our dressers were adorned with plastic Breyer horses and Teresa's horse show trophies. Outside of our daily barn chores we enjoyed playing outside, being with our animals (horse, goats, dogs and cats) swimming at the neighbor's pool, sledding, and riding our bikes. Dad liked to give us nicknames. Teresa was aka "Chookie" or "Poonie," and now "TC." Sharon was usually called "Searsie."

Sharon with Dad 1967

*Teresa & Sharon
ready to swim*

*Sharon & Tommy
on a goose chase 1968*

Teresa, Donna, and Sharon 1973

*Sharon, Donna & Teresa
May 1976*

*Teresa & Sharon at
Sadlon's pool*

Teresa on Gypsy with Dad & Cousin Eileen

Teresa & Miss Rich 1979

Teresa & Sharon with Missy

*Teresa & Sharon
(with Leo) 1976*

The Farmhouse

Our home was a simple four-bedroom farmhouse, painted white with black shutters with a front porch and a small garage on the side. By the side entry we had a bed of beautiful orange poppies, which came up every year, and in the front yard we had big maple trees.

Our house had one bathroom, which was downstairs, and always occupied. The kitchen and den were remodeled into one open space in the late '70s. We had yellow Formica countertops, maple wood cabinets, and a bar with four stools and old wood beam accents. We also had a small potbelly woodstove that would heat the kitchen on cold winter days. The original dining room was also remodeled into a living room with a brick hearth and larger woodstove. The parlor (as we called it) had a couch, upright piano, and a hi-fi stereo where we would listen to records, sing, and dance. There was very little heat upstairs so we would run down and stand by the woodstove to get dressed. One of the upstairs rooms was used for storage, which we called the "attic"—Mom stored everything there from Christmas decorations to Halloween costumes.

The cellar was cold and damp with a stone foundation and dirt floor. It smelled of sawdust and musty potatoes as we kept sawn pieces of baseball bats to burn in our woodstoves and a bin for our garden potatoes to keep them cool.

The Farmhouse when Dad bought it

Side of house and garage

Poppies by side porch

Pot belly stove in kitchen

The kitchen & bar

The Barns and Fields

Our farm occupied roughly 170 acres of land. A long dirt driveway led up to the property with a bridge that crossed over a creek. The driveway was divided into two sections: the upper part led to the house, while the lower part went to the barn. The barn was made up of two parts: the main barn, and the lower barn, also known as the "L." The haymow, where we stored hay, grain, and sawdust, was located on the second floor. The haymow was tall with huge wooden beams holding stacks of hay up to the rafters by the end of the summer. It was quiet and still with dangling cobwebs and smelled of a mixture of dried hay and sweet grain. There were wooden ladders on each section to allow you to climb up to the top to throw down the hay bales. They were scary to climb and you had to be careful not to fall. We had two silos on either side of the barn that stored silage (chopped corn) for the cows during the winter months. The pole barn located at the end of the "L" housed the heifers. Additionally, we had various outbuildings on the property. The garage was where we stored the trucks and tractors. Dad eventually built a large pole barn for his equipment. We kept the horses in stalls in the old garage and two smaller chicken coop-like buildings.

We had separate pastures for the cows and horses. The horses grazed in the upper pasture while the cow pastures stretched around the lower driveway, looping all the way around toward the woods and the crop fields, giving the cows plenty of room to roam and graze as far as they pleased. The pasture was scattered with cow pies (so

The horse barn

Aerial view of the farm

The new pole barn

you always had to watch your step) some fresh, others dried and flat like frisbees. The pastures were a mix of grasses, weeds, and wildflowers including burdock, thistle, goldenrod, milkweed, buttercups, and daisies. Some birds liked to make their nests in the pasture—killdeer would lay their speckled eggs in a nest hidden in a cluster of stones and weeds on the ground. If we got too close, the mother bird would squawk and fake a broken wing, trying to lure us away from her nest. Often, we would spot the tiny killdeer chicks darting through the pasture and sometimes we could even catch one in our hands.

Barbed wire fences surrounded all the pastures. Sometimes while crossing through the fences, the barbs would catch on our clothes, leaving a few holes here and there. In some areas near the barns, Dad installed electric fences. Once you accidentally touched an electric fence, you didn't make that mistake again! To test whether a fence was "hot," we would touch it with a long piece of grass or hay; we could feel a vibration without getting a shock. If it was quiet we could also hear the buzz of the electricity going through the wires.

The Milk House

Teresa in milkhouse 1976

Milkhouse in front of barn

The milk house, the heart of most dairy farms, was the first room you entered when walking into the barn. It is similar to the kitchen in a house. This is

where the day would start and end. In the center of the milk house was a large steel bulk tank that stored and cooled the milk. The milk would pour into the tank through pipelines extending throughout the barn. After milking was done, the pipeline would be flushed with a sanitizing liquid to rinse it out and prepare for the next milking. The milk house also had a small office nook where Dad kept receipts and papers about cow registries. There was a chair there where we would sometimes sit and procrastinate on our chores.

Every so often, the milk inspector would visit to inspect our farm. Sometimes we would get a heads-up from neighboring farmers that they were coming so we could hurry and prepare for their arrival. Everything had to be spotless: we used brushes dipped in a sanitizing solution to scrub all of the stainless steel to make it shine, wash the walls, and rinse the floor. We were all very relieved when it finally passed inspection.

The Cow Barn

Teresa & Sharon on "Amy"

View of inside of main barn

The cows that needed to be milked were housed in the main barn with rows of stanchions lining both sides. When you walked in, you could feel the waft of warm air and the smell of manure. In the summer we had big fans blowing to help circulate the air to keep them cool. In the winter we would let the cows outside in a fenced area after milking to get some fresh air and exercise. The barnyard was cramped and muddy in the offseason.

From spring to late fall the cows were turned out to pasture each night and again in the morning after milking. It was always a joy to watch them rush out to the fresh, green pasture for the first time in the spring. They would kick and leap with their tails in the air—a hilarious sight coming from such big, heavy animals.

When it was time to bring them back to the barn, all we had to do was call out, "come boss, come boss," a phrase that Dad had used for many years. We always assumed that he made this up himself, but it is actually an old expression that farmers have used for centuries to call their cows. It is derived from the Latin word for cow, *bos* and over time was shortened to "coboss." As soon as we called out to them, like clockwork, the cows would lift their heads and start making their way in. Some came running eagerly with their heads nodding and udders swinging with each step, knowing there was feed waiting for them. Others, especially the older ones, took their time, moseying along at their own pace. Over time, their hooves wore a web of dirt paths throughout the pasture leading to the barn. When they had all gathered nearby, we would swing open the big red steel gate, and they filed into the barn. Each cow knew exactly which stanchion was hers and would head straight to it without hesitation. Once they were all in place, we would hurry through the barn, locking them in by the neck. A few cows challenged us each time, refusing to go into the right stall. We carried around a wooden cane to help guide the stubborn ones back where they belonged. One of those troublemakers was named "Vera," but we called her "Blockhead" because of her big square-shaped head. She constantly tried to sneak into the neighboring stall to munch on someone else's feed.

Dad had a powerful whistle he used to round up the animals. Sharon was always determined to learn how to do the whistle herself and spent hours practicing it. She'd press her two middle fingers against her tongue and teeth, positioning them just right, to produce a sharp, loud whistle. It took countless tries and patience to finally get it.

Sharon's favorite cow was named Sarah, a mostly black cow with a few small white markings. As you entered the barn, she was the third cow down on the right. Sharon loved the name so much that she ended up naming her daughter Sarah, too. Tommy's favorite was a mostly white cow named Amy. We used to climb up and sit on top of her back; she was so calm and gentle, unphased by the extra weight.

As you can imagine, working in a cow barn is not a glamorous job. Sometimes the gutters would fill up with a mixture of rain and cow urine, which we called "deep pee water"; it smelled quite pungent. We would sometimes get splashed with it from the cow's tails or accidentally step into it, ruining our barn boots. One of the worst scenarios was getting plastered in poop at a moment's notice when the cows lifted their tail with explosive diarrhea! This was most common in the spring when they started feeding on fresh pasture grass.

The barn was also a dangerous place; you could get easily kicked by a cow when milking or get bucked with their heads (a big reason for removing their horns). You could also easily fall from the ladders in the haymow. One time Tommy threw down a bale of hay not knowing Teresa was just below trying to climb up the ladder. Luckily, she was not injured, but it was scary nonetheless.

The barn held plenty of fun memories too—especially the music. The AM radio was always blaring "81 WGY," filling the barn with the sounds of the '70s as we did our chores. We knew every song by heart. Tunes by The Carpenters, Paul McCartney and Wings, Carly Simon, Carole King—they became the soundtracks of our childhood. Even now, when we hear one of those songs it instantly takes us back to the farm. Dad listened to a lot of talk radio too, like Paul Harvey, a radio commentator who always ended his talk shows with "This is Paul Harvey, good day."

Once a year Dad would have the inside of the barn whitewashed to sanitize the walls and beams. It was a laborious process that required us to prepare the barn by putting away every tool, wheelbarrow, bucket, and piece of twine. If we left anything hanging on a hook, it would get covered in the bright white, chalky substance and we might never see it again. Once they sprayed the whitewash, the barn looked completely different, with everything in a shock of bright white and a chemical smell that would linger for days. In hindsight, we realize that this may not have been the healthiest environment for us to be in. With time the barn would gradually

View of farm from road

return to its usual state, which we (and the cows) preferred.

The barn phone was mounted on the wall just outside the milk house. We had a party line, so if we picked up the phone in the house while Dad was already on the line in the barn, we could hear his conversations and he could hear ours. This was especially frustrating when we just wanted to talk to our friends in private. Every now and then, we could even hear our grandmother's phone line. The phone was certainly not private in those days!

The Old Pole Barn

The pole barn was located at the end of the "L" structure and served as a home for the heifers—young cows. They were kept in a large pen where they could roam around freely. A haymow was located above the pen, and we would climb up a ladder onto a catwalk to cut the hay bales and throw them down for the heifers to eat.

Cleaning the pole barn was always a challenging and dreadful task. Manure would pile up high since it was only cleaned about once every couple months. We used the front-end loader of the old Farmall M tractor to scoop up the manure and dump it into the spreader. It took many trips back and forth to the field to unload. The fumes from the manure were so strong that they stayed on our clothes long after the work was done. We wore tall boots just to make it through the thick muck in the pole barn. Once the manure was finally cleared away and the clean concrete floor appeared, we would shake fresh straw all around. They were always so happy when you let them back into their clean pen; they were like little kids, running around and kicking, their tails in the air. After cleaning the pole barn, we were all starving and couldn't wait to stuff our faces with Mom's cooking. Dad used to say that manure and hard work makes you hungry!

View of Pole Barn from house

Chores

Living on a farm there was no escape from doing chores; they were an essential part of farm life. Farm kids had to work hard to help keep the farm running smoothly. We started working in the barn as soon as we were old enough to hold a pitchfork. We wore a dirt path with our boots on the hill between the house and the barn. Being in the barn was second nature for us. We had a long list of chores to do every day after school: throw hay bales down from the mow, fill the sawdust carts, fill the chutes with grain, scrape the manure from the cow stands, bed the cows with sawdust, feed them silage, grain, and hay. We also had to take care of the calves; feed them hay and pails of milk and clean their pens. The calves were fun to take care of, being so cute and playful. They would often get frisky and jump around in their pens. They also liked to suck on our fingers as if they were suckling milk from their mother; their tongues felt rough and our hands would be slimy and sticky afterwards.

After supper, we had to head back down to the barn to push up hay to the cows with a broom, spread fresh sawdust bedding beneath them, and clean up while Dad finished the milking. We disliked going back to the barn in the evenings because we had homework to do and TV shows to watch. Sometimes we would try to sneak out by climbing the side ladder up to the haymow and run to the house, hoping Dad wouldn't notice—but he always did. Just as we were settling in to watch *The Waltons* or *Little House on the Prairie*, Dad would call up to the house from the barn phone, looking for us, yelling "Get the hell back down here." So, we would go back to the barn, begrudgingly.

Sharon & Tom in barn 1974

Two calves suckling

Hill between house and barn

Horse pasture in winter

Dad plowing near the horse barns

Dad with Teresa 1977

In the winter months we had to feed and water the horses before school. We would haul large plastic buckets of water up the hill to the horse barn. The buckets would freeze and we had to chip away at the ice so they could drink. During the summer the horses roamed around the pasture and drank from the creek, which made our lives a lot easier.

Spreading the manure was a necessary, yet not so pleasant farm task. We would scrape all the cow manure into the barn gutters, which carried it around the barn and emptied it into a pile on the manure spreader. The manure spreader ran on a PTO (power take-off) that was hooked up to the tractor. When it was turned on, it would shower the field behind with a layer of warm, steaming cow poop. On a windy day, you had to be careful that it wouldn't blow back at you, so it was better to drive against the wind or suffer the consequences! It was cheap fertilizer for the field and completed the circle of life on the farm, helping the next crops to grow. The manure was difficult to spread in the winter; when the snow got too deep, we would leave it in a pile on the edge of the field. Often, we would plant seeds in these manure piles (which were super rich in organic nutrients) and would harvest cartloads of pumpkins each fall.

Dad with manure spreader early 60's

Aerial view of farm -manure tracks in field

Milking

Dairy cows need to be milked twice a day, 365 days a year. We milked around fifty cows and for Dad that was typically between seven and ten a.m. and again between seven and ten p.m. His schedule was much later than that of most other dairy farmers, who were either already out in the fields or off to bed at those times.

Occasionally, Sharon would take over the evening milking if Dad was busy with

Dad milking 1977

Dad chewing his cigar

something like baling hay. Milking was never an easy task. It involved a lot of bending, squatting, and moving in between cows, which takes its toll on the body after a while. To begin milking, you first had to clean the teats with an iodine solution before attaching the milking machine to the udder. Once the machine was in place, you had to keep track of time and gently palpate the udder with your hands to ensure the milk was fully drained. We had four separate milking machines and had to keep track of all four cows at once to ensure no machine stayed on for too long. After finishing with one cow, you would move the machine to the next and repeat the process. The whole process typically took about ten minutes per cow. Milking all the cows would take a couple of hours depending on the number of cows. Some of the cows were more difficult to milk than others and would resist and start kicking when the machine was attached, making the task even more challenging.

On occasion, a cow would develop mastitis (an infected milk duct) and require antibiotics. This typically happened after calving. Dad used a separate milking container for the sick cow's milk to ensure it didn't mix with the milk in the main pipeline. It would often be dumped or fed to the barn cats.

Dad would often milk late into the evenings. With the sun setting and the barn lights glowing, his cronies knew they could stop by to "shoot the bull." That would make us mad because it slowed down the milking process, which then delayed getting our chores done. We just wanted to get back to the house to finish our homework or watch TV before bed.

It was typical for Dad to chew tobacco or on a cigar while milking cows in the early days. Then he would often sit and smoke a pipe after milking. It was his way of relaxing after a long day. We loved the scent of the tobacco from his old pipe.

Sometimes, after finishing chores or working in the field, Dad would take a quick nap. He'd sit on a kitchen barstool nodding off with his chin resting on his chest. We liked to play a prank on him saying, "Dad the cows are out!" He'd awaken, startled, and then we'd laugh and say "just kidding." In no time, he'd be fast asleep again.

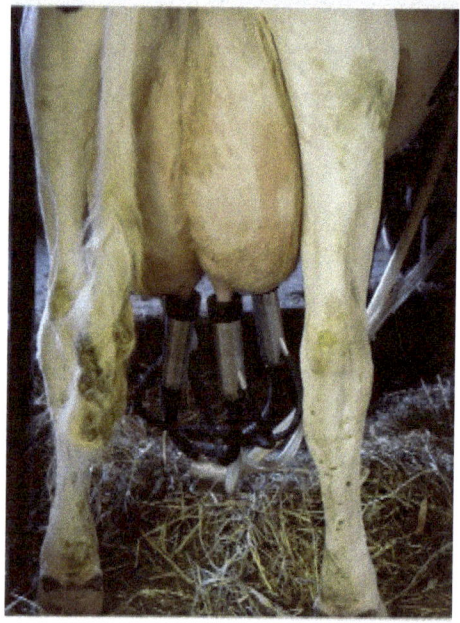

Milking machine

The Milk

Every other day, a large tanker truck would visit our farm to collect the milk we had produced. The tanker would then transport the milk to a nearby processing plant where it would be homogenized, pasteurized, bottled, and distributed to stores. Our payment was based on the quantity of milk in our tank and the current market price. The pricing process was complex and influenced by various factors including federal and state government regulations, as well as supply and demand. Sometimes, the price was so low that we would receive a check for zero dollars after taxes and fees were deducted. They would never know, week to week, what their paycheck would be. Mom would be discouraged, wondering how she would buy groceries that week. It was a constant struggle to make ends meet, but somehow, we always managed.

During the 1970s, dairy farmers went on strike because of the low prices they received for their milk. Dad was a part of the National Farmers Organization (NFO) and by going on strike they could hopefully score a higher price. For about one to two weeks, we did not sell any of our milk and instead dumped it down the drain. This must have been a difficult time for our parents since they were not getting paid.

We grew up drinking raw, unpasteurized milk. Whenever we needed more milk, we would head down to the milk house to the large stainless steel tank which stored all of our milk. It had a heavy lid that opened upwards and a large agitator inside that swirled the milk around to mix it and keep it cool. We would plunge our jug into the swirling white liquid, and scoop it up. After a while, we could see the cream settle on the top. Flies would commonly get into the milk tank, but we didn't pay much attention to them, we were used to it. We would just swish them away as we filled our jugs. The Creedon family, who had thirteen kids (three were our hired hands) used to come to our farm every week with their big bottles and fill them from our tank. We believe Dad must have given them a very good bargain.

Calving

On our farm we had Holstein cows. The Holstein is a popular dairy breed due to the large amount of milk they can produce. They are easily recognized by their distinctive black and white markings. Many of our cows would be bred with a Jersey bull, which was a smaller dairy breed thereby producing a smaller calf, which was easier for the cow to deliver. We loved the Jerseys because they were so pretty with their reddish coats and big long eyelashes. They looked like deer. We had one with the number 7 on its forehead that we convinced Dad to keep: one brown cow in a sea of black and white.

On the farm, we often had cows ready to calve, which was essential for them to start producing milk. Sometimes a pregnant cow would stay out in the pasture to give birth on her own, and we would have to go looking for her. We rode out on the three-wheeler or the horses to search for her. More often than not, she would hide far off under the bushes or trees to be by herself. On occasion we would come across a cow still in labor out in the field. If she appeared to be struggling, we would carefully approach, helping by gently pulling on the calf's legs during each contraction. We weren't exactly equipped for deliveries out there, so we just did what we could in the moment to assist.

Once we found the mother and her calf, we would drive out with a tractor and wagon to bring the baby back home, while mom trotted protectively alongside all the way to the barn. Mother cows are very protective of their babies, so we always had to be careful not to get charged at.

If the calf was born in the barn, we had more control over the situation and would regularly try to help the cow out. If the calf was breech, we would have to call the vet to turn the calf around inside the birthing canal. That was beyond our skill. The calving equipment was kept in the milk house and consisted of a long chain with a one-foot metal bar attached. This could be used to help pull the calf out of the birth canal by its hooves. Once the cow's water broke you would see the feet sticking out and could reach in and loop

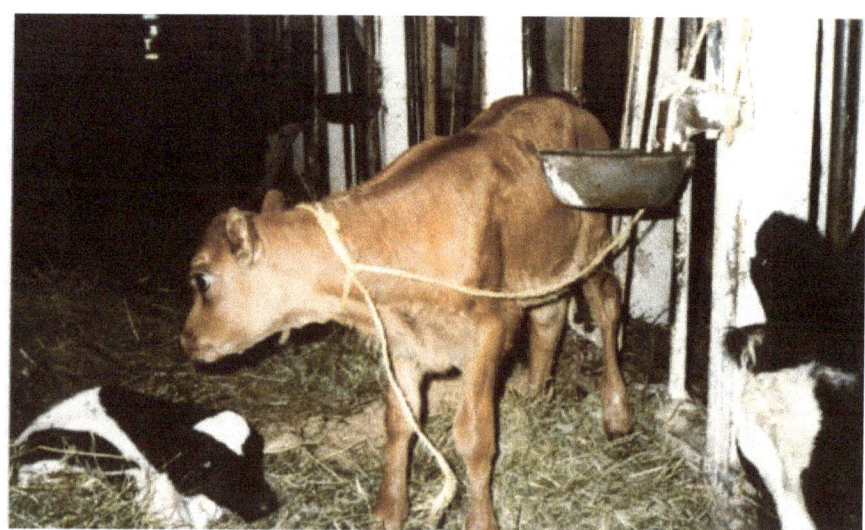

A jersey calf

the chains around them. Every time the cow had a contraction we would gently pull on the bar and chain to assist in the delivery. Once the head came out (which was the widest and most difficult part), the rest of the body would soon follow. If a calf wasn't breathing properly right after birth, Dad taught us how to clear the mucus from their airway by carefully sweeping our fingers across their nose and mouth. If the calf was still not breathing properly, he would tie a rope to its hind legs, fling the other end over a barn beam, and hoist the calf up and slap its chest. Once we heard the bellow, we knew the calf was going to be okay. Occasionally the calf didn't make it, despite our efforts. Dad would quietly take the calf away to be buried. This was a solemn occasion for us kids but also financially difficult for Dad.

Soon after the calf was born came the afterbirth: a huge mess of tissue, clots, and membranes that the cow would expel within a few hours or so. If allowed, the cow would slurp this down like a smoothie. It was the strangest thing to watch. If it was left to hang around, the dog would get at it and you would find it days later, strewn around the barn or yard stinking rotten.

It was important that the calves nursed from their mothers right after they were born so they could get colostrum from her milk. Colostrum is rich in nutrients and antibodies and is essential for the calf's health and immune system. After a day or two of nursing, we moved the calves to their own pen. The mothers would often bellow for their babies for a few days afterwards, and it was always a little heartbreaking to hear. But over time, they adjusted and life would move on.

One challenge was teaching the young calves how to drink milk from a pail. It wasn't always easy. We would straddle their necks with our legs and gently guide their mouths down into the milk while they sucked on our fingers. As they began to get a taste of the milk, we would slowly pull our fingers out, encouraging them to drink on their own. It often took several tries before they figured it out.

With cousins 1976

Veal Calves

We used to raise veal calves; only select bull calves were chosen for this special type of meat. They were housed in an old sawdust cart that had been repurposed to create a confined space for them. These restrictive quarters were aimed to produce tender, pale meat, which many consumers preferred. We also fed them a mixture of milk and raw eggs to make their meat more tender. We couldn't help but feel sorry for them, thankfully, we didn't raise many.

Veal calf

Milk Fever

Milk fever was an awful condition where a cow would suddenly just collapse within hours after giving birth. Dad said it was from the cow's calcium level dropping dangerously low from making so much milk. When that happened, Dad would pull out his large-bore needle and bottle of calcium gluconate IV solution. He'd locate the jugular vein in her neck and insert the needle. Once blood flowed, he'd connect the IV tubing, and we would help by holding the bottle up high—it took a long time and made our arms heavy and tired. Then, suddenly, like a miracle, the cow would awaken and stand up as if nothing ever happened.

Ketosis

Within the first few weeks after giving birth, a cow's energy needs skyrocket due to her increased milk production. If the cow doesn't eat enough to meet those demands, her body starts breaking down fat, producing ketones as a byproduct. When ketone levels got too high, it could lead to ketosis. One of the telltale signs was the cow's breath which had a distinct sweet, fruity smell. They would also have a poor appetite and decrease in milk production. Dad would call the vet, who would administer an IV (propylene glycol or dextrose) which would help the cow recover.

Bloated Bellies

Sometimes a cow would develop a condition called "bloat." You could tell because their bellies would be severely distended. Bloat results from the accumulation of excessive gas within the belly from fermentation. This can be a serious problem and can lead to death. If the cow was in a lot of distress, and the vet was not easily accessible, Dad would insert a trocar into her belly to release the pressure. You could hear the sound of gas seeping out and it smelled like rotten eggs.

When a cow was sick, sometimes Dad used a long stainless steel device to push a magnet down the cow's throat in an attempt to gather any metal that the cow may have ingested. The metal bits would then collect on the magnet instead of going along the cow's digestive tract where they could potentially cause a fatal puncture.

Dehorning

When the calves reached a certain age, small horn buds would begin to appear. Horns could become dangerous—not just for the people working with the animals but also for the other cows. To prevent future injuries, the horns had to be removed while the calves were still young.

Dad would gather a few of the hired hands to help with the dehorning process. It was a hard thing to witness. The calf would be held down firmly while the horn buds were cauterized with a hot dehorning iron, similar to a branding tool. It smelled badly of burning hair and flesh and the calf's cries made the whole experience even more unsettling. We dreaded watching this and were relieved when it was over. Fortunately, the wounds on their heads healed quickly and in a matter of days, you could barely tell anything had been done.

Butchering

Every year or two Dad would select a bull calf to raise for meat; we always called him "Bully." We would feed him well with pails of milk and hay and grain. Once he was the right age and size, Dad would have him put down and sent to the slaughterhouse. It was something that we dreaded as we always got attached to Bully and we never felt prepared to lose him. We knew we needed to let him go and over the years we got a little more used to the process.

Dad had a hired hand named Charlie. He was a short older man who wore a bucket hat and baggy jeans. Charlie helped with odd jobs around the farm and one of those was to butcher the bull. They would use a gun to shoot the bull "right between the eyes." Dad told us that one time the first shot didn't work (they only had one bullet loaded) and the poor bull ran around, stunned. They had to scramble to find more bullets to finish the task. After the bull was down, they cut the throat to drain the blood and used the front loader of a tractor to hang the animal up high. Once the blood was drained the carcass was cut into quarters and all unwanted parts were discarded; then it was brought to the slaughterhouse. A pool of dark red blood mixed with dirt would remain for days at the spot where it happened. We knew to stay far away when a bull was being butchered, but once, in a moment of curiosity, Sharon hung around and watched. That visual would stay with her for a long, long time.

We used to go with Dad to pick up our meat once it was ready. The slaughterhouse was cold and damp and smelled of wet concrete and blood. We would help load the meat, wrapped in white paper packages, which was put into the chest freezer kept in our garage. Whenever Mom needed to make dinner, we would reach into the freezer and pull out T-bone steaks, ground beef, liver, or any other cuts of meat she needed. We tried not to think about the fact that the meat we were eating was our "Bully."

The Vet

On a farm the vet was regarded with high esteem. Dad tried to care for sick animals himself to avoid the extra bills, but when he needed help, Dr. Schoonmaker was our trusted veterinarian. He would arrive in his pickup truck wearing a jumper and tall rubber boots, carrying a kit and a stainless steel pail. We would stand by and watch as he talked with Dad and tended to the animals. We thought that someday we might grow up to be vets ourselves and hoped to learn a thing or two, but he could be a bit stern and never seemed much interested in involving us kids. Nevertheless, Dad was grateful for his medical expertise and we were happy to see our animals recover.

The Breeder

Growing up on a farm, we learned about reproduction at an early age. We watched curiously as stallions mounted on the backs of mares and tomcats grabbed the necks of females as they growled and hissed. One time our German shepherds, Kurt and Missy, were oddly stuck together by their rear ends for hours. We couldn't imagine what was happening to them. Dad said not to worry, it was just something that dogs do when they're in heat. "Heat" was a common word used on the farm. "She's in heat" referred to a cow or mare who was ovulating and ready to mate or be bred. In a herd of cattle, a cow would jump up on another cow signaling she was in heat.

Dad would call the breeder, also known as the "artificial inseminator," to come by and work his magic. He would show up dressed in a jumpsuit and rubber boots. A metal tank of liquid nitrogen sat in the back of his truck and he would reach in and pull out an icy steel cylinder filled with little straws of frozen bull semen. Then he would walk down the rows of cows in the barn to look for the chalk marks that Dad drew on the cows' backs to indicate they were in heat.

The breeder arrived at work fully equipped with his insemination kit, which included an iodine wash, a long plastic glove that reached up to his shoulder, and a steel pipette that could hold one of the small frozen straws. Using these tools, he would inseminate the cow and if successful, she would give birth to a calf after approximately ten months. It's crucial that cows give birth every year to ensure continuous milk production. If they fail to do so, they are referred to as "dry." Farmers often resort to artificial insemination because keeping a bull around can be quite dangerous. Bulls can easily injure the cows and will trample anyone who gets in their way.

Hired Hands

Over the years, Dad had many hired hands on the farm—which we didn't mind at all, since it meant a little less work for us. Some of the memorable helpers were Jeff Carrig, Mike Marosek, Ron Deming, Rick Kneunle, Sean Gallagher, and the Creedon Boys—Ronan, Rich, and Pat. A few of them liked to tease us, tossing our hats around or pulling pranks to keep things lively.

We had a fridge in the garage full of Pepsi and Kool-Aid for the hired hands to help themselves when they needed a drink. Dad would often invite them into the house to eat dinner or enjoy a snack after they finished working. Sean would usually help himself to a big bowl of ice cream.

Jimmy Tibbitts (Tojo), was a regular at the farm; he lived just down the road from us. He grew up on a farm himself and always helped other farmers in the area with any chores that needed a strong back. He would often ride over on his three-wheeler to help Dad or just to shoot the bull. He was the neighborhood town crier; there wasn't any news he didn't know about. Tojo has worked for Burnsy for years and in many ways has been like family to us. He still helps Dad with fieldwork and odd jobs.

Many of our hired hands still stop by to see Dad, chat and reminisce about the old days. Some have even brought their children along to be hired hands too.

Ronan in haymow

Fixing roof- Sharon looks on 1980

Rick Kuehnle, Tommy & Sharon 1974

Tojo unloading hay

Dad with Tojo after unloading sawdust-1984

Dad with Tojo re-building porch

Tojo on golf cart

Jeff Carrig, Roger Tibbitts & Dad

Sean Gallagher with Mom eating ice cream

Fixing Fence

Every spring, we helped Dad repair the barbed wire fences that had taken a beating from the harsh upstate New York winter—sagging wires and leaning or broken posts were common after heavy snowstorms. It was no small task, with fences stretching around nearly every edge of our property. If the fences weren't secure, the cows would get loose and end up in the neighbor's field, or worse yet, on the road. Dad would buy large spools of barbed wire, new wood posts, and pails of metal staples. Many times, the wires would just be loose and need to be tightened up. We would use pliers to pull the wires taut then hammer in a new staple to secure it. But if the fence post was rotten or broken, it had to be replaced entirely. That meant driving a new post deep into the ground with a sledgehammer. This was heavy, hard work, and the barbs would dig into our skin. We needed to wear leather gloves to keep our hands from getting cut up. Dad would always comment when we drove past a farm that had tight, pristine fences, "Now there's a nice fence."

Picking Rock

In the spring, we would be summoned to go out and "pick rock." One would be perplexed by this statement: "Is that like picking corn or a tomato?" Not really. After a field was plowed to prepare for a new crop, the turning of the soil would bring up rocks hidden beneath the surface. The larger rocks had to be cleared away as they could damage the planting equipment and prevent seeds from settling properly in the ground. We loathed this job, it was dirty and dusty and it always seemed to be on the hottest day. We picked rocks as big as our little hands could handle and put them on the back of a wagon. We didn't even wear gloves and our hands would be sore and caked with mud. Sometimes giant boulders would turn up after plowing and Dad would have to pull them out with a tractor loader. Then we carted the rocks down to the creek and dumped them along the side. Over the years there was a pretty big pile lining the creek. These field rocks were probably similar to the ones we see lining pastures in New England and Ireland.

Planting

Each year, Dad planted corn, oats, alfalfa, and timothy. He started by using a moldboard plow to break up the soil and turn it over. Once the field was plowed, he would hook up a disc harrow to the tractor. Its round steel discs sliced through the clumps of dirt, breaking them up to create an even surface for planting. For crops like alfalfa, timothy, and oats, he'd make another pass with a spring-

Unloading oats 1977

tooth harrow drag. This leveled the soil, smoothing it out to form an even seedbed that crops needed to take root and grow properly. Sweet corn needed the soil to warm up to at least sixty to sixty-five degrees before it would start to germinate. To know when it was time to plant corn, Dad would take a long thermometer and push it three to four inches into the ground, checking to see if the soil was ready. When the ground was finally ready, he would attach the planter and fill it with seeds. The planter did the job of depositing seeds in a straight row across the field. He would also spread fertilizer along with the seeds to help them grow. After several days and hopefully some sun and rain the little sprouts could be seen poking through the soil. Before long, the field would transform into a sea of green. Dad always said the corn should be "knee-high by the Fourth of July" if it was a good growing season.

The oats were grown to feed our horses. In the fall, when they turned a golden color, they were ready to be harvested. We would often pick out the little oat seeds and chew on them, they tasted just like the oats Mom bought at the store. Dad hired a man named John Kazmierski to bring his combine to harvest them. The combine was an enormous machine (it would take up two lanes on a typical road) that stripped the oats off, leaving the rest of the plant in a row behind it. This would then be dried, raked, and made into bales of straw, which were used for bedding for the cows and horse stalls. The oats were blown into the big old dump truck and later put into feed bags, which we stacked and used over time. The horses loved their oats, and Dad would mix them with molasses to reduce any dust. Their muzzles would end up coated with the sticky sweet syrup.

Haying

Haying was typically done two to three times during the summer season. The first cutting, typically in June, was the lightest and made mostly of tall grasses like Timothy, which is preferred for feeding horses. The second cutting was richer and denser, composed mainly of alfalfa and clover. If the weather was favorable, there could be a third cutting, which would be similar to the second cutting. Dad was an expert at predicting the weather, which was crucial when making hay. Even a light rain or a heavy dew could ruin the hay, causing it to mold or rot. To ensure the most accurate weather forecast, he relied on a weather scanner and had the personal phone number of a local weatherman. He also would keep an eye on the neighboring farmers to gauge when they were going to

Raking hay

Baling hay

start their haymaking as it was a good indication of sunny days ahead.

Haying took multiple steps and careful planning. First, the hay had to be tall enough and ready to cut. Dad used his 806 Farmall, with his red and yellow New Holland haybine, to mow it down. After the mowing, the hay would sit in the field to dry for one or two days, depending on the weather. The drying grasses created a lovely, sweet smell that would permeate the warm summer air. One of our favorite scents is still fresh cut hay.

Once the hay had dried it was time to rake—usually Teresa's job. The hay rake had long spinning steel spokes that would turn over the hay into neat rows called windrows. It was important to collect every bit of hay and keep the rows straight, to make baling easier.

Stacking hay

Unloading the hay wagon

Summers in the field were usually scorching hot, with no shade to cut the sun's rays. After being on the tractor for hours, we had to be careful not to burn our fair Irish skin and back then sunscreen options were quite limited. The wind and sun from the fields left a distinct scent on our skin—we called it "sun arms."

Dad had a John Deere baler, and behind it he towed a wagon that could hold around 150 bales. The baler would kick the hay bale up in the air, and Dad would adjust the settings so it would land exactly where he wanted it to on the wagon. We would often run out to the field where Dad was haying to hand him a cold beer.

Once the baling was done, the fully loaded wagons were hauled down to the barn to be unloaded. A tall metal elevator carried each bale up to the haymow above. One by one, the bales were pulled from the wagon and stacked in the haymow. The hired hands working up there had the toughest job of all; it was usually stiflingly hot, easily over a hundred degrees, and thick with dust. On some occasions we were called to help in the haymow; afterwards we would emerge soaked with sweat and covered with hay dust, our cheeks flushed.

Unloading the wagon was a little easier than the haymow and you could move at your own pace. Our hands would be blistered from the twine and our arms were covered and itchy with scratches and hay splinters. Usually, after it was all done, we would all sit around in the warm summer night air, drinking Pepsi to cool off. The hired hands would be covered with sweat and chaff and Dad would tell stories, laughing and joking. Those were fond memories.

Sweet Corn

Every year, Dad grew a big field of sweet corn and we've been selling it since we were young kids. He has become somewhat of a local legend. Everyone in town knows about Burns Sweet Corn— it's the best and the sweetest. Every Saturday morning during the summer we would pick a truckload of corn and bring it downtown to the Little Falls Farmers' Market, which was held in the parking lot

Paths in corn field

Dad at Farmers Market

Donna in corn field

Pat Ward picking corn

behind the bank building. Typically, farmers there were selling vegetables, herbs, homemade breads, honey, pickles, and preserves. Sometimes there were a few unique crafters selling items like soaps, pottery, or jewelry. The Amish farmers would park their horse and buggy nearby as they sold their goods which became an added attraction for shoppers.

All the locals would gather around the back of Dad's old green Chevy truck to say hello and get their corn. Occasionally someone would complain about the price of our corn and remark that they could "get it cheaper down the road." We would have to respond with a smile and nod to avoid saying something we shouldn't! We also sold corn directly from the farm and customers would drive in our yard to buy a dozen or two ears.

Picking corn was hard work and took time to master. You learned to tell when an ear was ripe just by the feel of it. The cornfield was often blazing hot, and the sharp edges of the corn leaves would scratch up our arms and leave us itching by the end of the day. We carved paths through the cornfields as we filled up milk crates with corn and lugged them back into the truck.

We had a car that we nicknamed the corn car—a light blue 1960s Chevy that had belonged to Great Aunt Mary. We'd stuff the trunk and back seat full of corn until there was barely room to close the doors. We also rigged up the three-wheeler with milk crates strapped to the back, making as many trips as it took to get the job done.

From August to October, we ate sweet corn for supper almost every night, so by the end of the season, we were pretty tired of it. Over the years, we had different varieties: Butter and Sugar, Silver Queen, and then the Super Sweets. Dad would plant and test the varieties for the seed companies. The sweeter the better. The fresh young ears with small kernels would pop in your mouth, and with a little salt and some delicious Queensborough butter, it was pure heaven. Dad has been buying Queensborough butter from Canastota, New York for over fifty years. It's the best butter ever with the perfect texture and just the right amount of salt. We always had a tub in the fridge and we still do today.

Silage

Every fall, when the cornstalks started to ripen and turn light brown, Dad would chop the corn in the field to make silage for the cows. Silage is made from chopping up the whole corn plant—the stalk and the ear of corn—and then loading it into the silos to feed the cows through the winter months. We had two silos that were filled each fall. Fresh silage has a grassy smell, but it can be quite pungent and sour when it ferments. The fermentation process also releases toxic gases, which are dangerous to inhale, so we always had to be cautious around the silos.

Our hired hands would shovel the silage down the chute from the silo where it would land on a concrete slab.

From there we would scoop it up with a large pitchfork and load it into the wheelbarrows. In our second silo, we had

a mechanical silo unloader in place. We'd flip the switch to get it running, then place our wheelbarrows under the chute to fill them up. Then we would haul the wheelbarrows around the barn, dumping a ration in front of each cow.

Dad cutting corn silage

View from silo window

Dad unloading silage

Sawdust

There were two kinds of sawdust that Dad would regularly purchase to use as bedding for the cows. One was prickly and dusty and made from sawn-up baseball bats from a nearby bat factory. The other, which we much preferred, was

made of soft, curled wood shavings. Of course, the dusty kind was probably the cheaper option. It would feel gritty in our eyes and the dust would fill our noses so we would usually wear masks when we had to work with it. Dad used his big old dump truck to haul a load of sawdust from a nearby mill. Then, Dad would blow the sawdust into a big pile in the haymow, where it would sit until we shoveled it down into a cart below. Using a large shovel or wide pitchfork, we'd scoop it up and gently spread it throughout the calf pens and under the cows.

Wood Stoves and Wood Piles

We owned two woodstoves; the one in the kitchen was a potbelly stove, and the other in the living room was a Vermont Castings "Defiant." It could get so hot at times that the sides would glow red. One winter, we even had a chimney fire—it sounded like a howling wind and was scary. We used to clean out the stove pipes in the snow using a big stiff brush to remove the creosote that lined the sides. We burned a lot of firewood each year to keep the two stoves going. This required a lot of work gathering logs, splitting them and stacking the wood. We used a wood splitter that was hooked up to our tractor which made the job a bit easier. Sometimes Dad or Tojo would use an ax. It was our job to stack the wood—many cords of it. We stacked it in the back of the barn and then brought it into the garage where it could dry out.

Wood splitter and wood piles

The cast iron "Defiant"

Flies

Flies were a constant nuisance on the farm and difficult to control. They swarmed around the animals' faces and ears, leaving them to spend much of their day swishing the pests away with their tails. The cows and horses got clever, often standing behind their pasture-mates to let the others' tails do the work for them. Flies were especially common in the barn, and Dad would hang sticky fly strips from the milk house ceiling—they dangled like strings of raisins, catching anything else that got too close. We would often spray the horses down with fly spray before letting them out to pasture or before taking them out for a ride. The horses would get bitten by the dreaded green-headed horsefly, whose bite would cause the horse to kick or rear up. The flies would eventually end up in the house as well so we always had a flyswatter on hand. In the fall and winter as they died off, they would accumulate along the windowsills and Mom would suck them up with the vacuum. Mom said that as a toddler Sharon was caught once eating flies from the windowsill, perhaps thinking they were raisins.

Dad's Elevator Accident

Injuries are a common occurrence on a farm; farming is often considered one of the most dangerous occupations. One summer while haying, a large steel elevator fell onto Dad's leg. The elevator was a massive, heavy piece of machinery, requiring 2-3 people to maneuver it. Dad was rushed to the emergency room, where Uncle David, who was a doctor there at the time, stitched up the deep wound on his leg. It was a frightening experience and one of the rare times we saw Dad cry. Because of the injury, Dad couldn't milk the cows for a while and had to hire someone to come in, as we were too young to manage the task on our own. His absence from the barn was unsettling and we were all relieved when his leg healed and things were back to normal.

The elevator

The Creek

We had a creek that ran through the front of our property, our driveway had a bridge over it about halfway up. We didn't have to worry about giving water to the horses or the cows when they were out to pasture. On occasion, the creek would surge to that of a swift river after a heavy rain and it would rise up and over the bridge. One year, it happened so quickly that the horses were trapped on a tiny piece of pasture and we had to rescue them from the rising water. Sometimes it would reach the Kelleher's house at the other side of the pasture and flood their basement. We were sure glad that our house was on a hill.

Many kids have that one special tree to climb, and for us, it was the enormous Weeping Willow at the far end of our pasture by the creek. Its low, thick branches were perfect for climbing and finding secret spots to explore. The ground around it was well-trodden from the cows as they liked to sit under it on hot days to cool off.

Water rushing under the bridge

Creek flooding over bridge

Max running through the creek

The Knolly Piece

We frequently rode our three-wheeler and horses down the dirt road which wound along the fields to the back of our property. The road took you across a tiny creek up to a hilly field surrounded by big old hardwoods. We called the field "the Knolly Piece." We used to say "When I die, I want to be buried on the Knolly Piece." That is how special this field was to us. When we rode the horses, we would give them a kick and gallop them up the hill. You could hear and feel the thud of their hooves beating into the ground as we climbed. Then we would pull back the reins and turn at the top to admire the view of our farm below while the horses sighed and snorted to catch their breath. If we continued forward on the trail, it would take us all the way up to the woods, which signaled the end of our property.

We would ride the horses through the woods on a snowmobile trail that the neighbors made. If we wanted to, we could ride all the way to our grandma's farm on Cole Road.

Out in the fields, we enjoyed the challenge of making a grass whistle. We'd carefully search for a flat, sturdy blade of grass, press it between our thumbs, then blow through the narrow opening to hear the loud trumpeting whistle. It was a simple joy when it worked.

We remember one time singing "I'm Leavin' on a Jet Plane" by Peter, Paul, and Mary at the top of our lungs as we returned from a trip to the woods—climbing fences and running through the tall grasses. These memories might seem small and silly now, but they instantly take us back to those carefree days.

The road headed out to the fields

SECTION TWO

THE PETS

Our world revolved around our animals. We respected them, and gave them all a good life. If we weren't tending to them during our chores we were usually playing with them. They were a source of responsibility, love, and companionship.

Whenever one of our pets died, we would bury them beneath a big tree and etch their names on a sign so that over time we had quite a pet cemetery.

Our pet cemetery

Our Horses

We always had horses growing up. Over the years we kept adding more and more and eventually Dad ended up breeding his own line of registered quarter horses. They call them "quarter horses" because they can run the fastest quarter mile of any horse breed due to their muscular builds. Dad studied the horses' pedigrees and looked for studs that would have the best builds and dispositions. He liked them to be muscular with "big butts!" Poco Bueno was a favorite quarter horse of his. He loved to read about the big ranches like Four Sixes and King Ranch in Texas. We subscribed to *The Quarter Horse Journal* for many years. We liked to flip through and look for our favorites and hang them on our wall. Once Dad took us to Ohio for the American Quarter Horse Congress, which is one of the largest horse shows in the country.

Dad with Jericho, Star and Gypsy

Dad showing off their muscular butts

43

Cinnamon was our first, he was a Welsh pony the color of cinnamon with a big bushy mane like you would expect. He was a bit feisty and had a mind of his own.

*Moms classic headless shot
Sharon on Cinnamon*

Jess was a buckskin gelding (neutered male), he had a tan coat and a black mane and tail. He was big and frumpy with giant hooves and had the bumpiest trot. He also had a lot of energy so you had to be careful with him. Sharon had a close connection with Jess.

Sharon on Jess with Tommy

Goldie was a palomino mare with a golden coat and a white mane and tail. She used a hackamore for riding (a piece around her nose) instead of a bit in the mouth. She was Sharon's favorite. Goldie was always palling around with her buddy Gypsy.

Goldie

Gypsy was Teresa's favorite. She was a bay mare with a dark brown coat and a black mane, tail, and legs. She had a white star on her face and a small band of white on one of her hind legs. Although she wasn't registered, she was probably a quarter horse. Gypsy had a gentle nature and anyone could ride her "broke to death," Dad would say. Teresa rode her in the local horse shows.

Teresa on Gypsy

Jericho was a tall, skinny chestnut gelding with a pretty reddish coat and a white blaze on his face. He was green broke (not trained very well) and afraid of his own shadow.

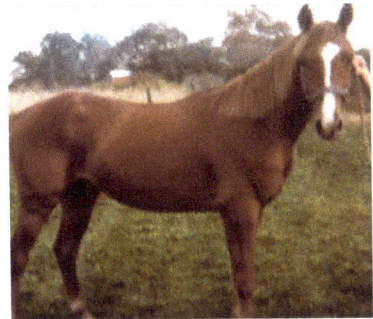

Jericho

Little Rock was a black mare and one of Sharon's favorites. She was a bit of a challenge to ride; she was only content while running full speed so you had to keep her under control and hold her back all the time.

Little Rock with Teresa

Sue was a bay mare who also produced some good foals. She liked to sway back and forth in her stall when she was bored; she was also a "cribber"

Sue

which is a nervous habit where a horse will chew on wood and suck in air.

Star was a bay mare and our prize broodmare; she gave birth to many of our favorite horses over the years. She was big and muscular and had a calm disposition. She had all the traits that Dad admired in his bloodline.

Star

Katie was Star's first foal. She had to be bottle-fed as a newborn because Star rejected her. She would rear up and start to kick or nip at her when she tried to nurse. We prepared bottles of formula using Joe Weider's Protein Powder (for body-builders) and raw honey around the clock. We developed a close bond

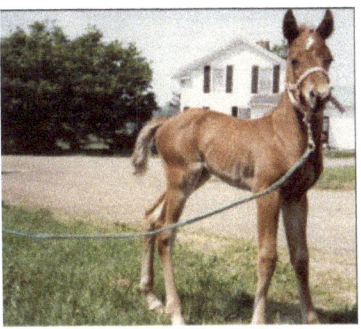

Katie

with her, but she ended up being spoiled and difficult to ride.

We would often ride out in the fields together with Goldie and Gypsy, even in the winter. We would call it "Velaminting" when we rode in the snow and could see the horses' breath. We also used to dress the horses up and put flowers in their manes and tails and hats on their heads. We would often skip the saddle and ride bareback.

Gypsy & Goldie with hats

Gypsy & Goldie

Teresa & Sharon Riding

Gypsy & Goldie with flowers

Bottle Feeding Katie

Mom with Gypsy and Starbuck

Horses in field

Mom with Katie

Gypsy & Goldie with cousin Chuck

Gypsy & Goldie with cousin Eileen

Horseshoes

Our farrier was Barb Gorham. She drove an AMC Eagle hatchback and was usually accompanied by her mother, who would wait in the car as she went to work trimming hooves and shoeing horses. Barb had weathered skin and straw-blonde hair and walked somewhat stooped. She wore a leather apron around her waist and had big, callused hands. She was thin and strong and would use her weight against the horse to prompt it to lift its hoof. She didn't so much as flinch if the horse started to kick or bite. She knew just how to handle them. We would only put shoes on the horses when Teresa was planning on showing. Otherwise, they would do fine as long as we didn't ride on the pavement. All of them needed their hooves trimmed and the frequency depended on how active they were. One time Dad took us to a horse auction and there was a pony whose hooves were curled right up like an elf; they likely had never been trimmed. The memory of that poor animal lingered in our minds.

Our Cats

We had a lot of cats on the farm, dozens of them. People would drop them off at our place and then they would just multiply. Mama Kitty was often pregnant, while tomcats prowled around, always waiting for their next opportunity. We would search through all the haymows looking for new litters. The mama cats would always find the deepest, most remote spots to have their kittens. We would listen quietly for

Fluffy Kitty

Leo

their soft mews, and when we found the litter, the kittens looked like baby mice—tiny balls of fur with their eyes still closed. Sometimes the mama would move her kittens one by one, lifting them gently by the neck to a new safer location. This meant we would have to search all over again.

Our grandmother, Gram Bam, loved coming up to feed the cats. She used to call to them by shaking the cat food and they would all run to greet her and gather at her feet. She was in cat heaven!!

The barn cats were excellent hunters, keeping the rodent population under control. They thrived on a diet of mice and milk, and they knew exactly when milking time was. As soon as we poured milk into a large pail, they'd come running, gathering around to drink their fill. Afterwards, they'd all head over to the air compressor in the milk house, where the warm air would blow over them like their personal hair salon, and they'd groom themselves clean. We called this "Footsie's Beauty Salon" after one of our favorite barn cats. Footsie was a gray tabby and our best hunter. Some of our other memorable barn cats were Funny Face, Lovey, and Miss Kitty.

Sometimes the barn cats would get very sick with distemper. This was a nasty respiratory infection where they would sneeze and their eyes would get crusted shut. Most cats that got this wouldn't make it. Of course, these cats never saw a vet—Dad could barely afford to treat a sick cow, let alone the barn cats. It was just the way it was.

Every now and then, someone would pull into our yard and park their car while one of the kittens, being curious and drawn to the warmth of the engine, would crawl up under the hood. As the visitor started their car to leave, a grinding sound would come from under the hood. Those moments were always heartbreaking for us and for the unsuspecting guest, who had no idea what was happening.

Some of the cats that we grew close to ended up living in the house: Miss Rich, Mama Kitty, and Fluffy Kitty were a few of the lucky ones. We couldn't help but think that the barn cats felt envious of them, seeing them curled up all warm and cozy in the house.

Sharon's favorite cat was named Leo or Lee-B. He was a huge Maine coon with long fur, one green eye, and drool often coming from the side of his mouth. He used to perch himself up on the wood pile and or the roof of the dollhouse. Sharon loved this big old cat and used to carry him around the farm. One day we were shocked to find him dead. We think he got the dreaded "circling disease" as we called it. This caused the cats to circle as if they were chasing their tail, then not long after, we would find them dead. Several of our cats had succumbed to this strange condition.

The saddest thing about the cats was population control. Sometimes Dad would ask the hired hands to collect the new litters and drown them in the creek; stuffing them into burlap bags and sinking them into the water with rocks. As sisters, we were the PETA people of

our time, staging a protest whenever we heard this was about to happen. We would rush down to the creek, making one final attempt to save the kittens. It never worked.

Momma Kitty and Miss Rich

Sharon & Tommy with kittens

Kittens in the window outside house

Gram feeding cats 1978

Our Goats

We acquired a pregnant goat named Twinkles from the vet down the road (Dr. Wainwright). She gave birth to a billy

goat we named Starbuck. He had black stripes down his face and curled horns. He had hair on his chin and two skin tags on his neck that hung like grapes. His knees cracked when he walked. He would lunge and buck if you weren't careful and he was very strong and rambunctious. He could break from ropes or chains easily and if he got loose, he would get into big trouble. We would find him in the oddest of places like the roof of a car or on the picnic table. Sharon would load Starbuck into the old corn car and drive him around the fields. He loved being a backseat driver and he would stick his head out the window.

Then there was Freddie the goat. He was a tiny, sickly little guy; sadly, he died shortly after we got him.

Starbuck on snowbank

Freddy the goat

Sharon and Starbuck 1979

Starbuck checking out the kittens

Backseat driver

Starbuck's favorite spot

Our Dogs

Missy & Kurt

Missy and Kurt were sibling German shepherds that we got as puppies. Missy was black and tan and Kurt was a mix of light and dark brown. They were friendly and loyal and so fun for us kids to be around. They were also good watchdogs and very protective of us. Both ended up with hip dysplasia. When they could no longer get around Dad had to put them down.

Most people, when they talk about putting down their dog or cat, they mean taking the animal to the vet to have it gently put to sleep by an injection. But not on our farm. Dad and his shotgun were our means of putting an animal down. Most of our dogs, and even some cows and horses, had endured this fate. It's just the way it was. Dad wasn't about to pay for the vet when he could take care of it himself. He believed it was the right thing to do.

Teresa with Kurt-1972

Teresa with Missy-1972

Tommy, Donna, and Sharon with Missy

Teresa with Kurt and Starbuck

Micky

Micky, a shepherd mix, was sweet and quickly became part of the family. He lived with us on both the Middleville Road farm and Cole Road after we sold the farm and moved. He used to get into fights with our Doberman, Max. Teresa was especially fond of Mickey and he became her pal when the rest of us left for college. He was known for sitting with his front paws neatly crossed.

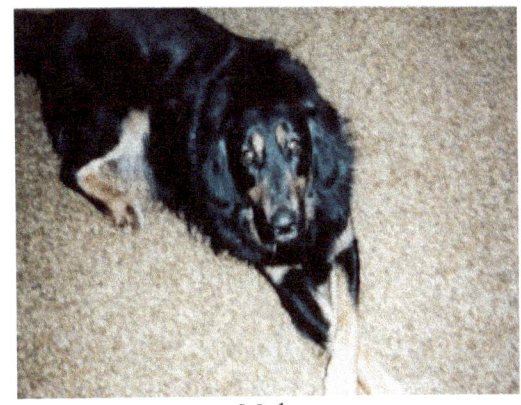

Mickey

Max 1 and Max 2

Max 1

Max 2

We had two Dobermans at the farm, both named Max. The first Max was red and had a mean disposition but somehow Sharon felt attached to him. We had to tie him up near the barn and he would growl and bark as people walked past. Max loved chasing cars down the driveway, which would eventually be the cause of his death. Max was biting the tires of the tractor Teresa was driving, and it crushed his jaw. He was badly injured and Dad had to put him down.

A couple of years later, we got another Doberman, this time a black one, and once again, named him Max. He started out as a playful puppy, but as he grew older, he developed a troubling habit of turning on people and biting. Eventually, we had to tie him up in the house to prevent him from starting fights with our other dog, Mickey. One day, Max attacked Mickey indoors, resulting in a bloody mess. Mom was screaming and tried to separate them. After Mom and Dad moved off the farm, it wasn't long before we made the difficult decision to put Max down; he had simply become too dangerous to have around.

Dooley

Dooley was a black and white Jack Russell terrier, much smaller than our other dogs. He was Dad's little buddy, often riding along in a milk crate on the tractor or sitting beside Dad while he ran his errands. At the bank drive-up, the teller would always send a Milk Bone through the tube just for him. Dooley had one ear that stood straight up; this appeared after he had a rabies vaccine. Dooley was definitely spoiled; every night at supper, he'd bark persistently until Dad tossed him a scrap from his plate.

Dooley on Tractor   *Dooley helping Dad plant corn*   *Dooley on Mickey 1994*

Henrietta

As we recall we only had one chicken. Her name was Henrietta, probably after the town where our Rochester cousins lived.

Unfortunately, Henrietta disappeared one day and it wasn't until many months later that we discovered her deep in the sawdust pile, all dried out. Poor Henrietta.

SECTION THREE
FAMILY LIFE

Farm Meals

Each day, we eagerly anticipated Mom's homemade meals. The day's hard work left us starving and the aromas of food cooking had us hurrying to the table. We always made time to sit down together as a family, and our conversations varied from silly to deep, and other times, the only sound was the clinking of forks on our plates. On an ordinary day, the four of us kids would eat at the kitchen bar while Mom and Dad would sit at the main table. If it was a special holiday we would all sit around the main table. Sharon was usually the first one done eating. Dad thought it was funny that she would use two fingers when eating and would lick them clean after each bite.

Mom made your typical family dinners: liver, meatloaf, cubed steak or T-bone steak, hamburgers and hot dogs—and they always came with some form of potato and a vegetable. Some of her other favorites were tuna noodle casserole, cream peas on toast, and Friday night fish sticks.

We had sweet corn at nearly every meal during the summer months. When she ran out of dinner ideas she would make us pancakes.

After dinner we would practice standing on our heads against the kitchen wall. We liked to see who could hold it the longest. Then we would go into the parlor to listen to our favorite records on the hi fi (like The Carpenters, Bee Gees, Olivia Newton John, and John Denver) and sing and dance before it was time to go back to the barn.

Lunch was usually sandwiches: cream cheese and olive, Velveeta, egg salad, bologna and cheese, or tuna fish. On weekends we'd have grilled cheese and tomato soup. We always had fruit to go with the sandwich and fruit cocktail was a regular favorite. Once Teresa stuffed her half-eaten Velveeta cheese sandwich into her thermos at school to hide it from the nuns (they would inspect our lunches to

Mom in kitchen

The kitchen table all set

The kitchen bar

make sure we ate everything). Mom sure had a hard time getting it out.

Breakfast was Cream of Wheat, oatmeal, Shredded Wheat, or poached eggs on toast. Mom would let us get the sugary cereals sometimes as a treat: Cap'n Crunch, Sugar Smacks, Corn Pops, Frosted Flakes, or Apple Jacks. Then she bought us Tang which we would drink sometimes instead of OJ. And of course, there were pop tarts. We had no idea that sugar was bad for us. They did such a great job marketing this stuff in those days.

Every spring, we planted a garden near the horse barns: potatoes, carrots, beets, yellow beans, squash, tomatoes, onions, and cucumbers. It was a lot of work keeping it watered and weeded. One of our least favorite jobs was picking the pesky potato beetles off the plants; we dropped them into jars of gasoline and watched them swirl around until they sank to the bottom. Dad would often ask us to head out to the garden at dinnertime to pick a few fresh green top onions to eat with dinner. He would dip them in a tiny dish of salt and crunch into them, raw. In the fall we would dig up the potatoes and store them in the cellar for the winter.

Dad's Dinner Time Discussions

Dad often took the opportunity at dinnertime to give us a lecture on various topics, usually offering some sort of life lesson. At the time we rolled our eyes in protest, but then we came to appreciate these lessons as we aged. He encouraged us to be more outgoing, embrace learning, and engage in conversations with wise adults. He wanted us to be our best selves and avoid "ending up on Furnace Street" a street in our hometown, which was his example of being less than successful in life. He admired people like our town physician Dr. Burke, Basketball Coach Hubie Brown and salesman Zig Ziglar (he has framed photos of them on his book shelf). He would always remind us to " say hello first" when approaching people. And when it came to friendships, he often said that most people will only have one or two "real" friends in life. We now know this to be true.

Birthdays

Mom always made sure that we had a special birthday celebration every year. Birthdays were simple yet had a personal flare for each of us and always included a birthday cake. In the earlier days, our mom would bake us homemade cakes, but as we grew older, we usually had a store-bought Pepperidge Farm cake. That was a special treat for us. Sometimes, we would invite a few friends from school over for a party, but mostly it was just our family, and sometimes grandmothers or cousins.

Mom often made jello to go with the cake, serving it in her beloved red Pyrex dish (which is still in the kitchen cabinet today).

Teresa's 6th Birthday 1974

Mom's Birthday with cousins

Birthday 1969
with Gram Bam

Sharon's 5th Birthday
June 1970

The beloved jello bowl

Sharon's 3rd Birthday-
June 1968

Birthday party with cousins

Ice Cream

After dinner we ate ice cream just about every night. It was delivered right to our house by the Schwan man, Larry. Schwan's was a frozen food delivery company which came to our region. They had a pamphlet where you could check off what items you wanted for the next delivery. Larry would show up every couple of weeks in his big yellow truck with doors filled with frozen treats. We would clack our spoons in our bowls when we knew he was coming to signal we were out of ice cream. We would often greet him out by the truck to look in and see what he had. The ice cream came in big plastic pails, several gallons in each; butter brickle, chocolate marshmallow, and chocolate fudge swirl were some of our usual flavors. He also had ice cream bars (Choco Pops), ice cream sandwiches, and Nutty Buddies.

We made up a silly game when we ate our ice cream: we would stir it up until it was creamy and say that we were having a party for an imaginary person, "Bobby Jimmy Carol." Then we would say we were calling him and his number was "123456789" and we would dial the numbers on the old rotary phone and pretend to talk to him. God only knows how we came up with that!

Thanksgiving

Mom's sister, Aunt Frankie, always hosted Thanksgiving at her house in Herkimer with Mom's side of the family. Although it seemed like a long trip as kids, it was only a ten-minute drive. Frankie was a smoker, and we hated how our clothes would reek of cigarettes by the time we got home—the smell lingered for a long time. We would pass time in the basement playing with their old toys, like an old GI Joe set and little military figurines. One year, we even played on an Ouija board

Thanksgiving at Aunt Frankies

*Aunt Frankie and Gram Bam
at Thanksgiving 1976*

down there with Gram Bam. We were scared stiff when the game piece began to move. Looking back, it's funny to think that Gram, a devout Catholic, would have been totally fine with such a game. She probably had no idea it bordered on the occult!

Christmas on The Farm

Christmas at The Farm was simple, yet always special. Mom hung all of the Christmas cards that we received on the wood molding in front of the parlor. We had a manger that sat on top of the Hi Fi and we loved to play with the figurines. Mom had a tall sparkly Christmas candle that she lit every year, it smelled like bayberry and cloves. We always had a real tree and we loved the smell of fresh pine. The tree was always covered in garland and gobs of silver tinsel. It was lit with big colored glass bulbs that would get hot so there was a protective decorative foil behind each of them to prevent the tree from catching on fire. It would get so dry in the house with the wood stoves that static would cause the tinsel to stick to our clothes and hair and the tree would lose its needles pretty quickly. After Christmas we would put the tree outside in the snowbank and the remnants of tinsel would sparkle in the sun.

Mom made sure we had presents under the tree each year even if money was tight. We didn't ask for too much but we always got the big Sears Christmas catalog in the mail each year and would circle the toys that we wanted. We found out later on that Mom would store all of our presents at Gram Bam's house. After we went to bed on Christmas Eve she would sneak out and drive down to pick them up. Mom used to wrap everything in different colors of tissue paper, maybe to save on cost. We got baby dolls, games, crafts, musical instruments (guitars, drums, horns) and new plastic sleds. Sometimes we would get record albums: Loretta Lynn, The Carpenters, Barbra Streisand and The Cowsills were a few memorable favorites. She used to tell us that Santa couldn't come down the regular chimney—since it was too hot with the wood stove always running—so instead, he would come down the make-believe fireplace she set up in the parlor by the Christmas tree.

In early years we would go over to Grandma Louise's house on Christmas to have dinner and see our cousins and open more presents. In the later years we would go for Christmas dinner at Aunt Gert's. Aunt Gert and Cousin Linda liked to buy the four of us the same gifts but in different colors: sleeping bags, comforters, hats or mittens. We would glance over to see what our sibling's gift was as we were tearing off the wrapping paper of our presents.

Mom's tissue-paper-wrapped gifts

Teresa showing off her new guitar

New sleeping bags

Christmas at Grandma's 1972

Christmas morning

Christmas Morning-Mom and the kids

Our "fireplace" where Santa arrived

Church on Sundays

Every Sunday, we went to St. Mary's Church in Little Falls and sat in our usual spot in the front left of the church. We were usually late because we had to finish our chores and change into clean church clothes. During mass, we kids would often start giggling over something silly, and soon the whole pew would be shaking. Mom was never amused, she'd give us a stern look that said "knock it off," without a word. Dad, being so tall, had the advantage of seeing over everyone's heads and would send a sign of peace to his buddies—usually a nod or a quick wave. After church we would stop at Railello's Store to pick up the Sunday paper, then head to White Rose Bakery where we each chose our favorite donuts, like jelly buns and vanilla fingers.

Over the years, several priests came to visit us at the farm. One time we even got Fr. Russo to ride on Gypsy!

Us kids before church

St Mary's Church

Mom dressed up for church

Fr Russo on Gypsy

Easter Sunday

Mom always made sure to dress us up on Easter Sunday—back in the early days, that meant hats and dresses. One of our favorite traditions was hunting for our Easter baskets, beautifully wrapped in colorful cellophane. They were always filled with goodies: a chocolate or white chocolate bunny, marshmallow Peeps, and

Easter morning 1966

On the way to Easter Mass

Our Easter baskets

lots of jelly beans. None of us liked the black jelly beans, so we saved those for our cousin Linda, who loved them.

Easter was always held at our house with Mom's side of the family: Aunt Frankie and Uncle Paul, Aunt Gert and Uncle Bud, along with our cousins Linda, Dave, and Gary. After dinner our aunts would try to rope us into helping with the dishes, but we would quietly sneak outside for a ride, timing it just right to miss the cleanup. When we finally returned, we were always met with a well-deserved stern look.

Catholic School

We all went to St. Mary's Academy Catholic School in Little Falls, from kindergarten through the eighth grade. Paying for tuition was most definitely a sacrifice that Mom and Dad made for us. We wore school uniforms which were plaid blue with knee-high socks, a white button-down shirt with a blue vest, and a little cross tie. In the later years they were plaid green with a yellow shirt. While we didn't love wearing uniforms, it must have made it much easier on Mom. Once a month we had "Hot Dog Day" at school. We ate hot dogs and fries for lunch and didn't have to wear our uniforms. We also had "McDonald's Day" and could pick out a cheeseburger, fries, and a soda. Fast food was a special treat for us then.

Donna and Sharon were in Brownies and would sometimes attend a meeting after school. On those days they wore a Brownie uniform instead of the usual.

We had a mixture of lay teachers and nuns at St Mary's. Some of the nuns were strict, and we could be reprimanded with a quick slap of a ruler or tug on the hair. Some of the memorable nuns were Sister Thecla, Sister Rialda, Sister Linda, Sister Carolyn, and Sister Genevieve. There was a song the kids made up about the nuns: *"Kill Peroxide, Kill Witch Linda, throw the Thecla out the winda, all we ask is that you let us have it our way, have it our way at SMA."* It was mean spirited, but in a way, it was funny too.

Every Halloween, the school put together a haunted house in the bathrooms in the basement of the school. You would go through the line, then put your hands into a bowl of something like soft noodles or peeled grapes, and they'd tell you it was a brain and eyeballs. It was both creepy and fun, and the suspense always made it seem much scarier than it actually was.

The public school kids used to come to our school on certain days for religious education classes. Sometimes we would find chewed gum stuck underneath our desks the next morning. They used to call us "St. Mary's Fairies" and in return we referred to them as "Public Pigs." It was a typical school rivalry but ended as the two schools combined in high school.

Every June, we had the St. Mary's Fair, which was a huge event for us. We would watch out the school window as they set up the rides in the church parking lot: the Ferris wheel, Paratrooper, and the swings. There were lots of booths with food and games, and we couldn't wait for school to let out so we could go.

Sharon, Donna in brownie uniforms

Donna, Tom, Sharon in uniforms

St Mary's School on right next to church

The Bus

We used to take the bus to school, and every morning, we'd peek out the bathroom window, watching for it. Once it made its way down the Chluses' road and reached Van Allens' house at the corner, we knew we had only a few moments to hustle down the long driveway and catch it. More often than not, we'd be running late, and Bob Kelleher, the bus driver, would wait for us while the whole busload of kids watched us hurry down the driveway with our coats and lunch pails flapping around. The older we got, the more embarrassing this became.

On rainy or snowy days, we'd huddle under the small tree at the end of the driveway, trying to stay dry. There were also days when Bob had to do a "double or triple route," which meant we wouldn't get home until much later than usual. We hated those days because it cut into our free time before we had to start our chores.

Sometimes we would get teased by the public school kids when riding the bus in our uniforms. The boys in the back of the bus would sometimes grab Sharon's winter hat and toss it around, laughing. We quickly learned to avoid sitting too far back on the bus, where the older kids hung out.

Bob always greeted us with a cheerful "Hi, Murphy" when we boarded the bus, but we never understood why he called us that. He also had an odd habit of using his keys to clean his ears while driving. He would occasionally yell at the kids if things got too rowdy, but for the most part, he was quiet.

65

Barn Clothes

We had quite a wardrobe in those days. Being mostly hand-me-downs and '70's attire we had an assortment of various striped shirts and pants and bucket hats coupled with our barn boots. We didn't care much about what we wore, and we certainly didn't know anything about brands or fashions. Sharon had a few favorites, like her denim hat and her orange "Dunes" sweatshirt. Whenever we needed repairs, Gram Bam would patch our pants or hem our clothes. Our clothes always smelled like the barn, so we had to change and bathe often. We would kick off our boots as soon as we walked into the house, trying not to make a big mess—but, of course, we always did.

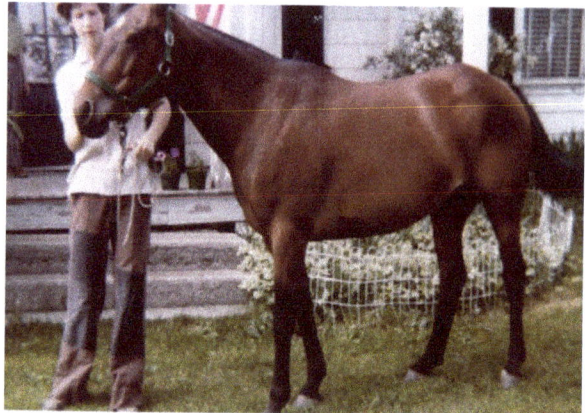
Sharon in patched pants with Gypsy

Getting Sick

During the '60s and '70s we had viruses like measles, mumps, and chickenpox. Mom's gentle touch always made us feel better. She would tend to us as we lay in the den on the couch, watching our console TV. She would put a cool washcloth on our heads and give us an orange flavored chewable baby aspirin or cod liver oil as was common in the day. Usually when we had a bad belly Dad's remedy was to "walk out to the gas tank and back and you'll feel better." Somehow he was often right, but if not, Mom would put a hot water bottle on our bellies which usually did the trick.

We would rarely go to the doctors when we were sick; most things were taken care of at home. But one time Teresa had a bad fever and headache for several days so Mom took her to see Dr. Burke. He asked her if the "light bothered her eyes." She replied no (even though it did) because she was afraid of him and afraid of what that might mean. Looking back now she thinks she had a case of viral meningitis!

One night, when Sharon was in fourth grade, she woke up to find her eyes were crossed, which was really scary. She went downstairs, and Mom had her lie on the couch to rest her eyes for a while. After a bit, Mom told her to go back to bed, as if that would fix everything. Later Sharon saw an eye doctor and was prescribed glasses. Thankfully, over time, her eyes corrected themselves and she no longer needed the glasses.

Sometimes we'd catch ringworm from the cows and Dad would spray us with something called Blu-Kote which was actually meant for livestock. One of its ingredients, gentian violet, stained our skin bright purple, and the color lingered for days. We would pretend it was from marker if anyone asked at school.

Bathtime

Typically, before bed, we'd all climb into the bathtub to clean up—farm kids tend to get pretty dirty. Sometimes, Mom would wash our hair in the kitchen sink. If we missed a bath, Mom would rub Rose Milk Lotion on us to help mask the barn smell. During the winter, our hands would get really chapped, so she'd have us rub on some Corn Huskers Lotion. One evening, when Mom couldn't bathe us, she asked Dad to step in. We remember him taking a washcloth to our bellies at the sink—he had no idea what he was supposed to do, and we didn't bother to correct him.

Donna, Sharon & Tom in tub

Tiny Pools

We had several small plastic pools over the years that Mom bought for us to use on hot summer days when we couldn't go to our neighbor's pool. The four of us would jump in and splash around, sometimes in bathing suits, other times just in our bottoms. It was just enough to cool us off.

August 1970 in just our bottoms

Bellies down in the pool

Little pool at Grandma's house

Trick-or-Treating

Halloween was always a bit difficult in the country, since we couldn't walk house to house to trick or treat. Instead, we often piled into the back of a car with the neighboring Chlus boys and made the rounds that way. Sometimes, we would stop at Grandma Louise's or Grandma Walker's houses. Our costumes were mostly handmade and passed down from sibling to sibling—so it wasn't unusual to wear the same outfit year after year. Sharon was a clown almost every Halloween, which is funny in hindsight, considering how much she actually hates clowns.

With the Chlus boys 1969

Halloween-1973

At Helen & Mary's 1975

Out to Camp

Our family never went on vacations or took many trips away from the farm. However, on occasion we felt lucky that we could get away for a few hours to visit Gram Bam's camp at Spruce Lake. It was only about a twenty-minute drive from our farm, but it felt longer. When we were there, we could swim in the lake, though it was always thick with lily pads, which made it tricky to swim around. Uncle Bud would cook hamburgers and hot dogs, and barbecue chicken on the grill for us. The camp didn't have running water, and we had to use an old outhouse, which always smelled bad. After Grandma passed, Mom's sister, Aunt Gert, bought the camp, and we didn't visit much after that.

With Mom in the canoe

*Tom, Sharon & Donna
lounging with Mom*

*Sharon and Tom floating
1977*

Teresa with her sailboat

*Grandma's Birthday
at camp*

Snowmobiles

We loved riding snowmobiles. Back then, we had a lot of snow every winter and everyone had one. Snowmobile trails were all across the countryside, making it easy to ride everywhere. There was a hill nearby they called "Killer Hill" which sounded scary; it was very steep and a challenge to ride on (but we never attempted). Dad often took us to the snowmobile races, about an hour away in Boonville.

Our snowmobiles were Ski-Doos. The "18" was an old-fashioned model with a rounded front. It didn't go very fast but we still had fun riding it. The other was the "TNT" which was newer and faster. Both would spew out exhaust right at your crotch as you drove along and you would smell like gasoline for the rest of the day. After riding, our fingers and toes would be frozen and our cheeks red and chapped.

Us four kids-1971

Dad with Sharon, Tom & Donna

Sledding down driveway 1976

Mom driving snowmobile

Teresa had a yellow Ski-Doo helmet, and Sharon had an orange Moto-Ski. We all had black, yellow, and orange wool Ski-Doo hats, as well as snowmobile suits and boots, which we picked out from the West Canada Creek Fishing and Hunting Store.

We would ride the snowmobiles out into the fields, sometimes making our own trails. It could get tricky when the snow was deep, and every so often we'd get stuck in a drift somewhere and then Dad would have to come pull us out.

Sledding and Skating

Our property had an ideal hill for sledding, which was right behind our house. We would slide down the steep hill and then walk back up repeatedly. We also went skating on the creek, carefully skating around the rocks. We used old white figure skates that had no insulation or padding, so to keep our feet warm, we'd layer on multiple pairs of socks. After skating and having fun outside, we would come back to the house and warm our frozen hands and feet near the woodstove. They would tingle as they thawed.

Storms

We seemed to have our share of big storms on the farm. Dad taught us how to read the sky, teaching us to sense when a storm was coming. Thunderstorms brought close strikes of lightning, often hitting the lightning rods, and once, tragically, killed a cow in the neighboring Tibbitts pasture. The cracks of thunder were so loud, they made the hairs on your neck stand up. Dad would sit in the garage, relaxed in a lawn chair, watching the storm while we would take cover somewhere in the house. We would count "one one-thousand" after each lightning strike waiting for the thunderclap, to estimate how many miles away the strike hit.

Winter was a tough time. Blizzards would often shut down the main road, allowing only snowmobiles to pass through the deep drifts. There were times when the temperature would be well below zero, freezing the water pipes in the house and barn. We layered up with our wool hats, scarves, and long johns. This was well before fleece or Gore-Tex. We'd wear a footpath with our boots, leaving deep tracks in the snow from the house to the barn.

If we lost power from a storm, Dad would hook up a generator to the tractor to keep some lights going. It seemed to happen, on more than one occasion, that we lost power just as *The Wizard of Oz* came on TV. We'd be forced to wait another whole year for the chance to see it again. We never had a tornado at the farm, but we were sure scared of them after watching that movie. Dad told us if there was ever a tornado, we should go to the southwest corner of the cellar, and stay there until the storm passed.

Clay Pigeons

A neighbor named Wayne Rockwell would come to the farm to shoot pigeons and starlings, as they created quite a mess around the property. We used to get so upset by it, not understanding why he had to do it. They deserved to live in peace like everything else. Dad had clay pigeons too that he used to practice shooting with his shotgun. Sharon tried shooting once and was excited when she actually hit one.

The Doll House

We had a tiny little log cabin next to the horse barns that we called the Dollhouse. It was our little hideaway, where we'd pretend it was our own house. We would bring in plastic cups and plates and pretend to serve a meal. Sometimes, we'd bring a cat or two along. Teresa decorated it with her favorite Bee Gees poster and set up a transistor radio.

Our Doll House

SECTION FOUR

EXTENDED FAMILY

Gram Bam

Our mom's mother was Grandma Edna Walker, also known as "Gram Bam." She lived alone for many years after our grandfather (Arthur Walker) died which was sadly just two weeks before Mom and Dad were married.

We have many memories of her coming up to the farm. She was a tiny lady, not even five feet tall. She was sweet, and quiet, and wore button-down sweaters, and fuzzy winter hats in powder blue. She liked to watch TV shows like *Bonanza*, WWF wrestling, and *The Incredible Hulk*. She liked to drink her tea VERY HOT; we called it "Gram style." She also loved sweetened condensed milk and our aunts would actually buy her some for Christmas—you'd see a gift under the tree in the shape of a can and knew that it was for her. Even us kids thought it was too sweet but she would scoop it out and eat it by the spoonful. She loved to play solitaire so much that the print on the cards was almost completely faded.

She had a bad heart and suffered multiple heart attacks. She kept a pill bottle of nitroglycerin on the arm of her couch. She would drive up to the farm several times a week; she lived just a few miles down the road on Monroe Street in "the city" in the house that she was born and raised in. Mom still calls the street she grew up on "Huddletown," a place where everyone knew each other and frequently visited one another.

Gram Bam never missed a birthday or celebration and she always came up to join us, usually with treats in hand for the cats. Sometimes she came up to the farm to lend Mom a hand with everyday chores, like washing our hair. They had their system: the ironing board was set up by the kitchen sink, where we'd lie down with our heads over the edge—just the right height for them to get the job done.

Sharon remembers once when she was very little, Gram had come to help Mom give her an enema. Panicked at the thought, she took off running to the top of the old metal slide in the yard, refusing to come down.

Gram Bam would get nervous if she stayed too late and she would check her watch often. Then she would say "well it's prit near four o'clock" and off she would go in her little tan car.

She would wave to us in the morning from her kitchen window as we rode the school bus past her house.

It was very sad when Gram suffered a stroke and had to move into a nursing home. We went to see her there but she was never the same and didn't even know who we were. Her house ended up being sold to strangers and we were sad that it didn't stay in the family. She died at age eighty-eight.

Gram Bam's Birthday 1974

Gram feeding cats

Gram Bam, Teresa and Max

Making a snowman 1970

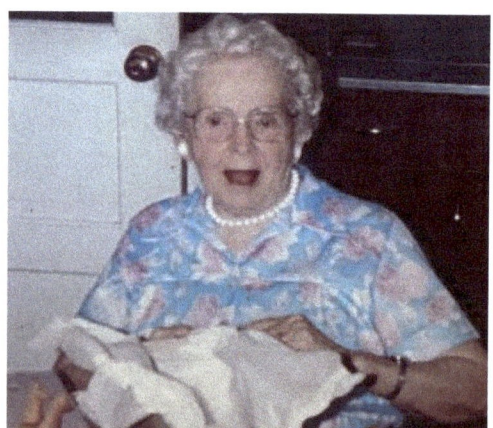

*Gram Bam
opening presents*

Grandma on St Patty's Day

Grandma Louise

Dad's mom was Grandma Louise Burns, also known as Grandma Louise. She was the matriarch of our family; our grandfather had died at only age fifty from a heart attack and she had to take care of everything after that. She was quite tall (maybe close to six feet) and fun-loving. She liked to stay up late and get up even later. She used to say "God love ya" and "Glory be" all the time. She was a hard worker and a great cook. Some of our favorites were her homemade chili sauce, chocolate mayonnaise cake, crab apple jelly (from the tree in the yard) and warm thick slices of homemade bread with butter. Dad loved her famous codfish gravy. We spent a lot of time over at the Cole Road farm with our aunts, uncles, and cousins who would often visit too. She frequently had a house full of people. We always went there for New Year's Eve and Christmas.

Grandma with Teresa and Sharon 1968

Uncle Joe and Aunt Ruth (Grandma's brother and his wife) would arrive at Grandma's on Sunday afternoons in their light blue Maverick, staying just long enough that Grandma would inevitably have to invite them to stay for supper. We'd all laugh about that.

In her final years, Grandma Louise moved away from the farm and lived with her sister, Aunt Mary, on Burwell Street after she could no longer care for herself. She passed away at the age of eighty-eight.

Sharon on Grandma's lap

Patrick Ward with Grandma Louise 1994

Grandma's birthday

Grandma with Teresa

77

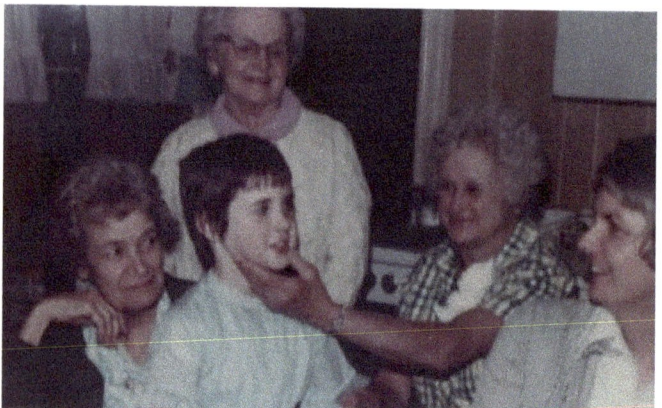

Teresa's First Communion with relatives

Teresa giving kisses

Aunts Mary & Helen

Grandma Louise's sisters were a big part of our lives. They lived together down in the city on Burwell Street, but they frequently made the trip up to visit us.

Aunt Helen ("Aunt Onnie") was fun and she liked to play, joke around, and tease us. She got sick with cancer and after a while got very frail and jaundiced. She passed away at Grandma's house, right there in the living room. She was the first in our family to die, and her loss left a deep sadness over all of us.

Aunt Mary ("Mimi") was quite a character. She was fond of gin and tonics and loved everything Irish, proudly dressing in green from head to toe every St. Patrick's Day. Mimi was a former school teacher and had a habit of writing notes in thick red crayon, just like she did at school. She loved to play "The Hokey Pokey" on the record player and dance around in a circle with us. She was very religious; she prayed the rosary often and always had the mass on TV when we visited.

Once, she joined us on a trip to Cape Cod with Dad's sister Mary Jo and Gram Louise. The moment we pulled out of the driveway she began saying the rosary out loud, which made for a very long trip. At the beach, she covered herself with towels to shield her fair skin, which burned to a bright pink in the sun.

On Sundays, we often stopped at her house after church and she would make us "club breakfast" with coffee, toast, bacon, and eggs. Her specialty dish at every family gathering was a jello mold. Mimi passed away at age ninety-one, the last of her generation.

*Teresa with Grandma
and Mimi*

*Helen, Grandma &
Mary 1977*

*Mary & Grandma
being silly*

Aunt Mary "Mimi"

*Mimi pretend smoking-
Dad, Aunt Kathleen,
and Tommy*

*Donna, Sharon
& Tom
wrestling Helen*

Aunt Helen

Cousins

Our cousins were a big part of our lives and we could hardly wait for their visits. Every November, they came to celebrate Grandma Louise's birthday, and the whole family would gather for a special dinner out at a restaurant. They also visited in the summer and at Christmas. Each year we'd take a family photo in the parlor to mark the occasion. They stayed at Grandma's for several days at a time and we'd spend those visits playing games, goofing around, and making memories. In the winter, we would sled down the steep side hill on the old wooden toboggan Dad used when he was a kid. Sometimes we had sleepovers at Grandma's, staying up late, eating popcorn, and telling ghost stories. We always felt like that old house was haunted as so many of our relatives had died there over the years. In the morning, Grandma would make us her famous homemade silver dollar-sized pancakes.

Cousins in MaryJo's MGB

Christmas with the cousins

Cousins on the hill at the farm

Playing games with cousins

Cousins visit at the farm 1981

Grandma and Mary with the grandkids

Family Gatherings

We frequently hosted extended family or neighbors at the farm for picnics or dinners. It wasn't unusual for people to simply drop by, stay for hours, and more often than not, Dad would invite them to stay for a meal. The air was filled with storytelling, and we would often eavesdrop on the adult conversations, which seemed so important and mysterious to us at the time. Sometimes, they'd play cards well into the night. Pitch was a favorite, accompanied by lots of laughter.

Visiting Grandma

Party at the house

Picnic with relatives

Picnic with the neighbors

Dinner at Grandmas

Christmas at Grandmas

Neighbors and family picnic 1978

SECTION FIVE

NEIGHBORS & FRIENDS

Our neighborhood, often called "Eatonville," was filled with a vibrant group of characters. They were kind, authentic people who always looked out for us and became an integral part of the memories that shaped our childhood. We had a few friends in the neighborhood, like the Chluses and Van Allens, and we'd often get together for birthday parties or to ride horses.

The Kellehers

Sharon on horse with Ruth Ann

Ruth Ann with us kids July 1966

Bob and Marion

Bob Kelleher

The Kellehers were our neighbors down at the end of our driveway. Their daughter, Ruth Ann, used to babysit us when we were little. Bob Kelleher was a stout man with white hair that he wore greased back. He ran a garage where they would work on tractors. Bob used to drive our bus for many years. Bob's wife Marion was a tiny woman who wore scarves on her head and smoked like a chimney; she would wave her cigarette at you as she drove by.

Dad still recalls the day, on April 17, 1983, when the big dump truck was backed into the haymow, and the back wheels went straight through the floorboards, nearly crushing the cows below. In a scramble, Dad asked us to run down to the Kellehers to borrow some tools to help pull the truck out. So, we ran down the long driveway and knocked on their door. Marion let us in and we quickly explained the situation, saying what a mess it was. Well, Marion took it to mean that her house was a mess, and she immediately apologized for the state of her kitchen. We felt bad that she misunderstood, but at that point, there was no correcting her. We left feeling mortified, and to this day, we still chuckle about it.

The Sadlons

John and Rose Sadlon lived just down Middleville Road up on a hill across the road from our pasture. John was sweet and kind. He was a big, burly man who rarely wore a shirt or shoes and was always tan, making him look like a big brown bear. He spent most of his time working in his garden or sitting by his pool. Rose was heavier set, with glasses and gray hair, and she had a bit of a stern demeanor, so we were always a little afraid of her. She was a good cook, and sometimes she would make us her special raspberry carmelettes to take home. In the evenings, the Sadlons would sit on their front porch, one at each end, watching over our farm from their hill like hawks.

Burns kids ready to swim 1972

Rose & John with us kids

Dad floating

Burns Farm in background

Pool cookout with the grandmas and aunts

Sharon, Donna, and Teresa

John with umbrella up 1973

1977 at pool

With Pinky Rasha

In the summer the Sadlons gave us an open invitation to come use their pool. We would walk or ride our bikes over. John had a special signal to let us know it was okay to come—he'd open up his pool umbrella, which we would eagerly watch for from our bathroom window. On some particularly hot days, he seemed rather slow at getting that umbrella up and we would wait and wait for what seemed like an eternity for the signal. The pool wasn't the cleanest; at times John would let the algae get out of control and the sides would be bright green, though it didn't seem to deter us.

They had two dogs: a basset hound named Bridget who was old and slow and a terrier named Scottie who barked and ran around a lot. John was always muttering and fussing with them. John swam a lot; he would tread water for a long time in the deep end and spout water from his mouth. Rose usually didn't go in the pool; when she did, she would only swim on the surface to avoid getting her hair wet. She was a very graceful swimmer. Sometimes Mom and Dad would come over, as well as our aunts and grandmothers.

Rose and John had grandkids that would sometimes come to visit: Laurie and Pinky Rasha. Pinky was the fun one. Laurie was more quiet and shy, and they talked a lot about her being carsick from their trip. It was a treat when they were visiting. One night Dad got a call from Rose that John was sick. Dad rushed over to their house. We don't know the details but John died that night. When Dad came back, he was very quiet. Things were never the same after that and we didn't go over to the pool as much. Rose lived alone for a while in that house until eventually, years later, she moved to New Jersey to live near her son.

The Chlus's

Mitch and Mary Chlus had a dairy farm up the road from us. Mary is our mom's best friend and over the years, they spent hours chatting on the phone. Being a farmer's wife herself, Mary could relate to all the ups and downs of farm life, and their shared experiences created a bond that lasted a lifetime. The Chluses have always been a special part of our lives.

In the early days, we would go trick-or-treating with their boys, David and Danny, and they would often join us at neighborhood picnics and other gatherings at our house. Mary is one of the best cooks around and we always looked forward to her homemade favorites, like her apple pie and fresh baked bread. Mitch is fun-loving and liked to joke around with us kids. Their lifelong friendship has been a true blessing for Mom and Dad.

Mom and Mary Chlus
early years

Mom & Mary

60th Anniversary,
Aug. 2021
with the Chlus's

The Salamones

Sam and Mary Salamone lived a couple of miles down the road. Though they weren't farmers, they were close friends of our family and the Chluses. Sam was a deacon in our church and, on occasion, would come to say mass for our family. He was a deeply holy man, and we would gather around to listen as he shared intriguing stories about miracles, places he had visited, and extraordinary things he had witnessed. Sam became sort of a spiritual advisor to us. His presence was calming and inspiring, and he played a meaningful role in our lives, even celebrating Teresa's and Martin's marriage ceremony.

Sam & Mary Salamone

Carmen

Carmen was a neighboring farmer also nicknamed the "Mayor of Eatonville." He was thin with dark, slicked-back hair and one arm with a prosthesis and a hook on the end, which we were very afraid of. He lost his arm in an accident on his farm many years ago. He was boisterous and loved to chat with Dad at milking time. He also liked to boss us kids around which we didn't appreciate. Carmen lived with his sister Patty. One time we stopped at their house and Patty offered us Italian anise cookies—which we promptly spit out when walking back to our car, as they had a distinct licorice taste that we weren't so fond of. Carmen held a neighborhood picnic in the summer which was a big event for all the farmers and families in the area. He would set up picnic tables in his pole barn and around his yard. We got to hang out with the neighbor kids, eating and playing games, such as tug of war. Carmen continues to call and shoot the bull with Dad.

Spotsie

Spotsie was an older neighbor who often stopped by for a visit. He'd help Dad out with odd jobs, running errands, and picking things up. Always dressed in suspenders and a fedora-style hat, he drove a worn-out blue Mercury. His face was deeply wrinkled, and he had a broad nose. Most of the time, he was drunk. With a lisp, he'd sing us the song "Sweet City Sue." He genuinely cared for us kids, and we didn't mind his visits—except for the times we'd catch him peeing on the side of the driveway.

Spotsie

The Gulley's

The Gulleys lived a few farms down from us next to the Tibbitts' farm. They had a sky-blue farmhouse with yellow trim. Bud Gulley was one of the hardest workers you'd ever meet. He was a slender man with weather-tanned skin, dark hair, and big callused hands. His wife Gwen was also a very hard worker; she wore rubber barn boots, jeans, and a brimmed hat over her strawberry blond

Bud milking cows

Gwen driving tractor

hair. We would see her frequently out in her garden. Both were very private people and dedicated farmers. Their kids Kara and Mark would sometimes come by to play, or come to our birthday parties, in the early days.

The Tibbitts Farm

The Tibbitts farm was just two farms down from ours. The Tibbitts Farm had a pasture that was just adjacent to ours, separated by a barbed wire fence. There was a row of trees and bushes on their property that we made into a fort. We called it "Tibbey Land". We used to play "Cowboys and Indians" and pretend that the mounds of rocks were Indian burial grounds.

Jimmy (" Tojo") Tibbitts has worked for us for many years. On the 4th of July, he and his brother Whitey would let off 1/4 sticks of dynamite in their yard that probably blew out half of their lawn. We'd often hear Tojo's mother call him home, "Yoo-Hoo, Jimmy!" she would yell from the house and he would hop on his Honda 3-wheeler and race down the driveway for dinner. Roger and Gary Tibbitts, Tojo's cousins grew up next door, they were both legally blind. Roger worked for our Grandmother milking cows for several years. He would be seen driving his tractor down the road since he couldn't see well enough to carry a driver's license.

Carly

Dave Carlson was another farmer up the road from The Gulley's. He was a wiry man with long hair, a ponytail and a long beard down to his chest; an original hippie. Dad said that he used to be a teacher but was fired after he refused to shave his beard and cut his hair. That's when he decided to go back to farming instead. He was a kind, quiet man and a very hard worker.

Carly-unloading hay

The Millingtons

The Millington farm is just up the road from the farm on Cole Road. The Millingtons had seven boys and one girl. Grandma Louise often said, "call the Millingtons" whenever something needed fixing or we needed help. They were always ready to lend a hand. Most of them still live nearby and continue to support our parents, often stopping by to visit. It was a great loss when their father, Don, passed away. He was a well-respected farmer and a good friend to Dad.

Millington Boys 1971

Dad with Don 2009

Skip

Skip was a big, burly man with black hair, a beard, and glasses. He used to ride into our yard with his truck or Arctic Cat snowmobile, typically in the evenings during milking time. He enjoyed hanging out and chatting with Burnsy. Skip used to hang onto the barn beams with his big, muscular arm. Sadly, Skip died in a tragic car accident. We had heard that two of our hired hands were with him that night, but we never learned about any other details and no one spoke about it ever again.

In costume at Little Falls Centennial 1970

Ron Trask

Ron Trask was a horse dealer from whom Dad bought many of our horses. He was short with messy black hair, thick black coke bottle glasses, and a beer belly. When he spoke, he usually had a bit of spit on his lip. He'd show up in our yard driving his makeshift horse trailer—a pickup truck rigged with a tall cap on the back. We never understood why Dad trusted him, but we ended up getting some of our best horses from him.

California Crew

Every summer the Mucica family from California would visit the farm. Mom went to school with their parents Bob and Marianne. They would show up all tan and in the latest California styles. We were intrigued by them and, admittedly, a little jealous. Still, we loved showing off—giving them a taste of farm life. They always seemed so amazed.

Mom giving tour of the barn

In the barn with the Mucica girls 1974

Neighboring Shops

Mike Sekerka owned a small farm store nearby. He was another farmer neighbor who had a habit of showing up right around milking time. He was a short, heavyset man who wore denim overalls and a hat that resembled that of a train conductor. He would lean on the sawdust cart while we worked, usually getting in the way. Sometimes he leaned too hard and the cart would fall into the gutter and we would roll our eyes. Mike sold farm supplies like shovels, pitchforks, and staples. He also carried jeans (which we called Sekerka jeans), barn boots, and cases of soda. Dad bought all our Pepsi from there.

Ed "Chink" Creedon owned a tire business up the road which was a real convenience for the local farmers. Dad would often stop by to get tires repaired for his farm equipment. We would duck down in the back of the car, hoping to avoid being spotted by him. Chink had a reputation of greeting people with a big sloppy kiss, and we preferred to avoid that kind of attention. Chink also sang in our church choir; he had a powerful, distinctive voice that was instantly recognizable. Chink would also drop by our farm regularly to buy fresh milk.

Bob and Marge Sperbeck ran a small grocery store down from the tire shop. They sold everyday essentials, and had a deli counter where you could buy some cheese or meat. We appreciated their ice cream cooler and would reach in for a frozen treat. Bob and Marge were odd people and not exactly friendly. One day, our bull broke loose from the pasture near their house and ended up tearing up their lawn. Bob was furious with Dad, even threatening to sue him for damage. They had a strained relationship after that so we didn't visit the store very often.

The Windy Tavern was a small country pub that was just across from Creedon's Tire Shop. Locals would drop by for a drink and chat with their neighbors. In the winter, it wasn't unusual to see folks riding their snowmobiles there. We have memories of Dad taking us there once while he drank a beer.

SECTION SIX

OUR PERSONAL MISHAPS, STORIES & REFLECTIONS

(Teresa)

My Broken Arm

One day I rode Cinnamon while my brother Tommy led him. I have a picture of that day, my little face smiling. Somewhere down in the lower driveway, Cinnamon let loose and bucked me off. I remember climbing up the back hill behind the house, crying. Mom took me to see Dr. Burke. I had broken my left wrist and he put me in a white plaster cast. I was in kindergarten then and remember banging the cast against my desk. When I got it taken off several weeks later my arm was shriveled and smelly. I blame Tommy for not holding onto Cinnamon a little tighter that day; he still insists that I jumped off!

Teresa on Cinnamon May 1974

(Teresa)

The Bike Accident

*Donna, Sharon, Tom
with our bicycle*

I had a vintage '70s banana seat bike with high handlebars, one gear, and a back pedal brake. I rode it up and down our long dirt driveway all the time. It must have been the *Little House on the Prairie* episode when Mary went blind that inspired me to ride with my eyes closed that day. I rode right over the side of the bridge, grazing the barbed wire fence and smashing my head into a pile of rocks that lay below. My bike floated downstream while I climbed back up to the driveway above. I yelled and cried for Mom to hear me, but so did our neighbor Bob Kelleher who proceeded to run after me as I ran up the driveway to the house, blood streaming down my face. I had never seen Bob run before, or ever again. My siblings went down to fish my bike from the creek. Fortunately, I had no broken bones and no stitches were needed that day. The bike made out okay too.

(Teresa)

The Barn Yard Incident

One day, while I was in the barnyard, a protective mama cow with her calf nearby charged at me and knocked me to the ground. Her large hooves barely missed my chest. Though I was stunned, I managed to escape without serious injuries. That experience taught me to be more cautious around mama cows.

(Teresa)

Stitches

While playing in the barn underneath the sawdust cart, Tommy pushed the cart over me not realizing I was there. I had cuts on my forehead and chin. Mom rushed me down to Dr. Burke's office in our red 1960's Chevy. There was a snowstorm that night and the roads were icy. Mom said many years later that she just "held the wheel tight and prayed" that night. I remember Dr. Burke putting a big needle into my forehead to put my stitches in. I still have those scars.

(Teresa)

TNT

One time there was a storm, and the Ski-Doo TNT was parked outside of the milk house with the skis frozen solid in the ice. I came up with an idea to pull it out with our truck. I hit the gas, the chain pulled tight, and the TNT lunged forward with the skis curled under it; it was a mess of twisted metal. I was horrified! How would I tell Dad what I did? Dad was quite forgiving about the incident, but that was the end of the TNT.

(Teresa)

Gypsy

Gypsy was a horse that Dad bought for us when I was in the fourth grade. I showed her in the Herkimer County 4H shows in classes such as western pleasure, pole bending, barrel racing, and trail and halter class. I won a lot of ribbons and trophies over the years, some blue. Gypsy qualified for the state fair one year. It was expensive, though, to go to a show like that. We didn't have a horse trailer to bring her to the shows. Dad rigged one up on the back of his pickup using metal gates. No one else came to the shows with their horse stuffed on the back of a pickup; I felt embarrassed. The Morris boys had a nice double trailer and shiny equipment and silver on their saddles. We had old used equipment that I polished in hopes of making it look show worthy. The night before a show there was a lot of preparation for Gypsy: she would get a

bath, shampoo and conditioner on her mane and tail, and we'd paint her hooves black, shave the whiskers on her muzzle, and clip the tufts of hair on her fetlocks. She looked so shiny and clean.

I would practice for the shows in a self-made dirt ring out in the hay field. I rode her any chance I could get. I enjoyed taking her out into the fields to ride along the fences and tractor paths where it was safe without woodchuck holes, I would let her rip and gallop fast. Sometimes I would meet my friend Sharon Carney on

Teresa riding Gypsy in corn field

Teresa at Horse show

Teresa at 4H Horse show

Shells Bush Road, cutting through the pastures so we could ride together. My teenage years weren't so bad because of Gypsy; whenever I felt stressed or upset, I could count on her to make me feel better. Gypsy lived until I graduated from college. She had a condition called "heaves" when she got older, kind of like COPD or asthma. She coughed a lot and got so thin you could see her ribs. I had asked Dad to put her down before she suffered. Then one day, I got the call that Gypsy had died. I felt grief like that of losing a close family member and cried for days. Later on, I learned that Gypsy had died naturally in her stall. I was angry that Dad had let her go on so long, but then I felt a peace knowing she died on her own terms. She was buried in the field across the road.

(Teresa)

Jericho

I bought Jericho for three hundred dollars with my own money that I had saved over the years. Jericho wasn't well trained. He was easily spooked: without notice he would suddenly lunge himself to one side. You had to hold on and be alert for this at all times. One day while riding up near the woods, Jericho got spooked and I fell off. He proceeded to run all the way back home. I hobbled to the barn and found him back in his stall, shivering and covered in sweat. The reins were dragging on the ground and the saddle, half-cinched, was sitting sideways on his body. We ended up selling him to someone that could train him better. I felt bad letting him go but it was the right decision.

Jericho

(Teresa)

Driving

Dad bought us a three-wheeler (Honda ATC) which was such a blast to have on the farm. I loved riding it around the yard and fields. I would sometimes get into trouble flipping it over on the hills or getting it stuck in the mud. I also drove the Cub Cadet lawn tractor around everywhere and would tow a small wagon to give someone a ride or pick up things along the way.

Dad owned red tractors: Farmalls. We had gas tanks right in our yard, one with diesel and one with regular gas. We could just pull up and fill up whenever we needed. Dad taught me how to drive at an early age, as soon as I could reach the

Teresa with the cub cadet cousin Eileen in wagon 1976

Teresa on 3 wheeler- May 1977

"Tina" the bulldozer

Dad on the Farmall "B"

Teresa on tractor

Dad gassing up the 806

pedals. I loved to drive and was very good at it. I could haul a wagon, back up a trailer, and rake hay. I even learned how to drive Dad's big dump truck up and down the driveway, shifting the gears. We also had a bulldozer named "Tina" that I drove around, pulling on the levers. This was big, dangerous equipment for a little girl. Mom must have prayed a thousand Hail Marys watching me. I also drove the old corn car on the dirt roads to go out to pick corn. Dad always said "use your mirrors" when he taught me to drive a car; it was one of the most important parts of being a good driver. When it came time to get my driver's license it wasn't a difficult task; I already had years of training.

When teaching my daughter Maggie to drive, she learned right away about using her mirrors too!

(Teresa)

Putting Down

Mickey was old and sick and when it was time to put him down, Dad asked me if I could help. My first response was, "No thanks" but then, dutifully, I agreed. We got into the truck; I drove as Dad held his shotgun beside him in the passenger seat, Mickey was in the back. Dad pointed to the spot where we would bury him near a row of trees, and we dug a shallow grave. Then Dad called Mickey to jump down off the truck. I closed my eyes and covered my ears and waited. When I heard the shot fire I looked up and Mickey was lying in the grass. Dad tied a rope around his feet and dragged his body to the grave. Tears streamed down my face as clumps of dirt covered his black fur. Dad and I rode back in silence; that scene would stay with me forever.

Mickey

102

(Teresa)

Tomboy

I thrived on the farm. I loved being with the animals, driving everything, exploring the creek and fields and riding the horses. I also liked to build things. Once, I made Mom a birdhouse with so many nails sticking out that a bird never dared to perch on it. I could do anything just as well as any boy and I tried to prove that to Dad. I followed him around and was his little helper, handing him a wrench or hooking up a wagon. In second grade Mom had my hair cut in a new, shorter style, so short that I looked like a little boy. In my first Communion picture I looked odd with my super short hair wearing a light blue dress with knee-high white socks. Nonetheless, I don't think it bothered me at the time. I sure preferred my barn clothes to dressing up. That's still true today. Nothing makes me happier than throwing on my jeans and

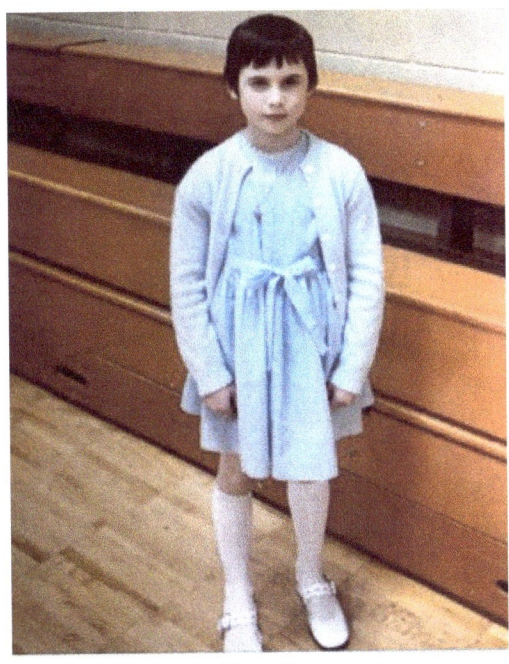

Teresa's First Communion

baseball hat to work in the garden or ride on my lawn tractor. It brings me back to those carefree days on the farm where I could be my authentic self.

(Sharon)

Little Rock's Adventure

One of my favorite horses was a spirited mare named "Little Rock." One fall afternoon, I took her for a ride out in the upper fields. The ride was peaceful and calm and the air was fresh. As soon as we rounded a corner by a tree line, a large woodchuck suddenly darted out of the brush, startling both of us. Little Rock

reared up on her hind legs in a panic. Before I could regain control, I was thrown off, and I hit the ground hard. The shock of the fall left me stunned for a moment and I felt like I could barely move. Shaken and sore, I decided it was best to walk Little Rock back down the hill to the barn. The unexpected encounter had startled both of us and I didn't trust her enough to get back on right then. But once my body healed, I knew I needed to get back on the saddle as soon as I could, determined not to let that define our relationship.

Sharon hosing down Little Rock

Sharon riding Little Rock

(Sharon)

Rats

One of the creatures I hated most on the farm was the rat. There was nothing remotely appealing about them—huge with long, ugly tails. Tojo, our hired hand, found it hilarious to throw a rat down the silo shoot while I was below, filling the wheelbarrow. I'd hear a squeak, then look up to find a rat on my pitchfork. It was usually alive, squirming around, but sometimes it had suffocated after being buried in the silo. I'd scream and run, so angry at him for doing this.

Occasionally, I'd find rats in the grain bin. We'd enter through the haymow and shovel grain down into a chute. Below, you'd place a bucket at the end of a funnel with a steel sliding door. Sometimes, I'd see the rats fall into the chute and freeze, too scared to open the door. I remember once slamming the flat steel door shut, just in time to trap a rat midway. The body was stuck while I pressed harder on the door, unsure of what to do next. I felt defeated no matter what. If I let go, it would leap at me, but if I kept pushing, it would be crushed in half! To this day, I still sometimes have nightmares about rats.

(Sharon)

Peepholes

One night, I started hearing a tapping sound coming from the wall next to my bed. After a while, I noticed a small crack in the wallpaper. When I looked closer, I saw a tiny bird's beak trying to peck its way through the drywall. It must have gotten trapped between the walls, desperately trying to escape. I decided to stuff the hole with tissues, day after day, until the tapping stopped, and I could no longer hear or see the bird. I figured it had either found another way out or given up. But a few days later, I sadly realized, from the awful smell in the room, that the bird had died in the wall. Poor thing.

(Sharon)

Chipped Tooth

One day, while I was in the barn, Tojo was busy fixing a cow stanchion with a sledgehammer. I happened to be in the wrong place at the wrong time when a chip of wood flew right at me. It struck one of my front teeth and sliced through my lower lip in one sharp blow. The pain was instant, and I could feel the blood starting to trickle down my chin.

They rushed me down to see Uncle David. He practiced medicine at that time through Little Falls Hospital. He assessed the damage and said I needed several stitches. But then he suggested I skip the novocaine. "It'll numb your lip for too long," he said, "and make it hard to talk or eat." I wasn't sure about his reasoning, but I trusted him—until the needle went through my lip. I clenched my fists, biting down on my lip to keep from screaming as he pulled the needle through. It hurt like hell. I had a scar there for a long time, a reminder of that unlucky moment. Later, the dentist had to file down my front tooth to make it even with the other one. My teeth were never quite the same.

(Sharon)

A Kick in the Arse

I'll never forget the day I sassed off to Dad. He called up to the house from the barn phone, asking me to come down and do my chores. When I refused, he didn't waste any time coming up to the house to get me. He was furious! He followed me through the kitchen and into the living room, where his boot finally caught up with

105

my behind. Before I even realized what had happened, I was crying. The sting didn't hurt as bad as my feelings had. I knew I was being fresh, and definitely deserved a lesson that I wouldn't forget. It's funny to look back on it now, but at the time, I sure wasn't laughing.

(Sharon)

Curls

My childhood was shaped not only by life on the farm but also by my curly hair. The older women would often comment on how beautiful my curls were and how much money they spent on perms to get curls like mine. But back then, I wasn't so sure curly hair was such a blessing. On school nights, I'd wear a wool hat to bed, hoping my curls would calm down by morning. One of our hired hands used to joke that bats loved nesting in curly hair— I believed it for a while. By high school, my hair had an even tighter curl which I wasn't happy about. Mom would take me to Aunt Mary Jo's to get my hair cut, probably because it was free. Looking back, I think if she'd encouraged me to grow my hair longer, the curls might have loosened up. It felt like everywhere I went my curls became the center of attention. Uncle David would always greet me with a little riddle: "Shar Shar La Pierre with the curly curly hair." At school, someone gave me the nickname "Spongy," which stuck through high school and even into college when returning for class reunions.

Besides my hair, I was also the tallest girl in my class for most of my elementary school years. People always asked if I played basketball. In high school some of the boys started calling me "Big Bird," which drove me crazy. Dad would say, "Sticks and stones may break my bones, but names will never hurt me," but I didn't agree. However, over time it stopped bothering me, and I think it made me more resilient. It wasn't until my forties that I started to embrace my curls, and now, I can't imagine myself without them.

Sharon, kindergarten far left 1971

3rd grade

Senior Portrait 1983

College portrait 1985

Teens to Twenties

(Sharon and Teresa)

As teenagers, we loved talking on the phone with our friends. The only phone in the house was located in the kitchen near the stairway. Thankfully, it had a long cord that we'd stretch to its limit so we could close the door at the bottom of the stairs—our only shot at a private conversation. Still, everyone in the house always seemed to know who we were talking to, and since we had a party line, Dad could pick up the phone in the barn at any time and listen in. If one of our friends happened to call and didn't start with, "Hello, Mr. Burns," Dad would get upset. To him, that recognition was important. He always taught us to say hello first when greeting others. We were naturally shy, so this wasn't easy for us. We'd have small conversations with visitors to the farm, but we weren't always comfortable with it. Dad, on the other hand, was known for being outgoing and talkative. When we rode around with him, we'd often sit in the car, sighing and rolling our eyes because he would take so long chatting with people. We couldn't wait for the day we'd get our own licenses.

As we got older, we'd spend sunny afternoons sunbathing on the front lawn, slathering ourselves with baby oil so that our fair skin often ended up burned. On weekends, we'd rush through our chores so we could spend the rest of the night hanging out with friends. After chores, we'd shower to get rid of the barn smell, then pile on makeup and hairspray as was the trend in the '80s. We didn't want to miss the high school football and basketball games or parties "up on the roads," where we would gather around a bonfire and sneak a few beers or some Boone's Farm wine.

We had a big party for our high school graduations. We got tables and chairs from the church hall and set them up in our pole barn. We had crock pots of meatballs and tiny hot dogs, baked ziti and cold cut platters. We invited neighbors and relatives and later in the evening our high school friends would show up. They were sure happy that Dad had bought a keg of beer for the event.

We ended up on similar paths after high school, majoring in animal science in college at Cobleskill and then Cornell. We didn't end up becoming veterinarians, but it sure seemed like the natural career choice for us. We lived together for a few years after college in Syracuse, New York, before going our separate ways and forging our own paths. We both ended up in New Hampshire where we live today.

Teenage years- with Dad

Teresa-getting ready to go out

Sharon getting ready to go out

Sharon's Senior Prom
1983

Teresa, age 17, 1986

Sunbathing on lawn

*Teresa's Junior
Prom 1985*

New Years at Grams 1983

Sharon's High School Grad 1983

Sharon's High School Grad Party

Mom & Dad's 25th

Teresa's Senior Portrait 1986

Teresa's High School Grad party

Sharon's College Graduation 1988

Teresa's College Graduation

Us kids with Mom

Selling the Farm

(Teresa)

It became more and more difficult after Sharon and Tommy left for college. I was stuck doing most of the chores by myself. Dad was tired too and oftentimes he would fall asleep in the chair while taking off his boots. He could no longer make ends meet and the debt piled high. He realized he couldn't keep the farm going anymore. At that time, the federal government had something called The Whole Herd Buyout Program or The Dairy Termination Program where they would buy out a farmer's dairy cows in an effort to reduce the surplus of milk in the country. Dad tried to sign up, but the price that they were offering was so low that he decided to sell our cows at auction instead. It was a very sad time for our family. I was glad to be off at college when the cattle trucks came. Not long after that, Dad put the farm up for sale. We ended up selling it to a couple from Connecticut, the Georges, who were retired school teachers. They had always wanted a farm and we were happy that they did a nice job maintaining it. We went to see it years later and they gave us a tour. They painted the house yellow and the barn red. It looked nice. They also made a big pond up at the Knolly Piece with a dock and a rowboat. They too could see how special that field was! It would change hands two more times. An Amish family bought it after the Georges and as we write now a Mennonite family lives there. It looks quite different now. We only wished it had stayed in our family.

SECTION SEVEN

THE LATER YEARS

Sharon's Hired Hand

In 1983, after I left for college, Dad hired a neighborhood boy named Patrick Ward to help with haying and barn work. Patrick lived just a few miles away and would often ride his three-wheeler over to the farm. At the time, he and his friend, Dave, were working at other farms nearby. When they heard that the Burns family had three daughters, they rode over together on their three-wheelers to see if Dad needed help.

One weekend, when I was home from college, Dad casually mentioned that Patrick had been asking about me. He added, "Patrick would make a good husband for you one day." I rolled my eyes; Patrick was almost five years younger than me and felt more like a little brother at the time.

When I came home after college, Patrick was still working on the farm. We started spending more time together—riding horses, picking sweet corn, and talking. Slowly, something shifted for me. He was handsome, witty, and funny, but also grounded and hardworking. Despite his age, he was more mature than most eighteen-year-olds I knew.

Teresa Maid of Honor

Sharon with Dad

October 9, 1993

Sharon and Patrick at the farm

Then, on New Year's Eve in 1989, at a party, he kissed me on the lips at midnight and told me he loved me. Not long after, we started officially dating. Four years later, on New Year's Eve 1993, he proposed. We were married that same year. Teresa was my maid of honor, and Donna and Tom were in the bridal party.

We welcomed our first daughter, Megan, in 1998, and our second, Sarah, in 2000. Patrick is the love of my life, and we've been together ever since—celebrating over thirty years of marriage. I'm forever grateful for my childhood on the farm—it not only shaped who I am, it led me to the life I share with my husband today.

Cole Road

The Farmhouse on Cole Road

Farmhouse in Winter

After selling the farm on Middleville Road, Mom and Dad moved to the Burns farm on Cole Road, a place where Dad and three generations of the Burns family were born and raised. It is nestled into the hillside with a sweeping view of the valley. Dad converted the cow barn into horse stalls and raised quarter horses there for several years (until the early 2000s). He brought over the horses we had at the old farm and they produced several foals over the years. When the time finally came to sell them, it must have been incredibly emotional for Dad to let go of the horses he had loved and cared for so deeply.

He still grows fields of hay, which he sells to farms across the Northeast, along with acres of his famous Burns Sweet Corn. Since 1997, Dad has also been selling oil for Central Petroleum Company (Cen-Pe-Co) to farmers and trucking businesses in upstate New York. He continues to recruit hardworking hired hands to help keep the farm running.

Aerial view of the farm and property

Cole Road Barn 2007

Sunset on Cole Road

Raking hay with Millingtons

View from the hill

Dad at haytime 2009

Burnsy at the corn stand

Dad feeding hay to horses

Hired hands with Dad 2016

Dad 2016

Dad's Signs

Dad checking the hay on the hill 2009

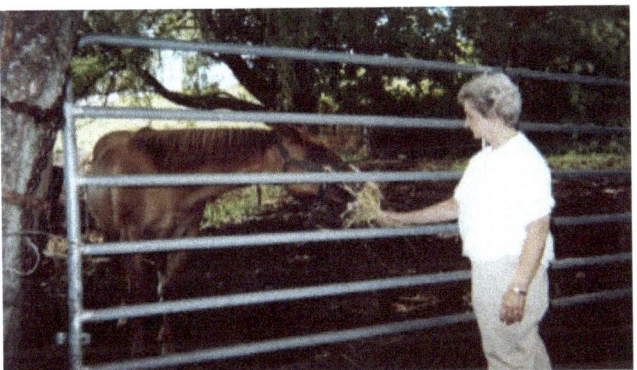

Mom feeding the horse

Mom weeding her flower beds

50th Anniversary Aug. 2011

Mom & Dad 60th Anniversary 2021

Dad with water buckets

Dad's horses in the field

Dad on 3-wheeler with Mom

Dad's Cen-Pe-Co award

Dad and Mom at Cen-Pe-Co conference

Sweet corn is ready

Burns Quarter Horse sign

Dad at the parade

Mom in the kitchen

Burnsy resting in his office

Mom on the porch- May 2021

Family Reunions

Family reunions have been a cherished tradition for the Burns family; we have had a few of them at Cole Road over the years. During these reunions, we cook out and enjoy plenty of sweet corn. One year, we even had a corn shucking contest, which Dad won hands down. We would also take a hayride during the reunion to one of our favorite destinations "Skunks Misery," a dirt road that winds through the countryside and features steep hills and a rickety wooden bridge. During one of these hayrides, our cousin Eileen filmed the journey with commentary, and on another occasion, our cousins played their fiddles. The neighbors must have gotten a kick out of all the ruckus.

We owned a big black antique car, a 1936 Buick, which we would take turns riding in up and down our road. Afterward, we took a big family photo on the hill with the car. It was commonplace for us to have a mass service at the farm, usually in the parlor or on the side lawn under a tent. A Jesuit priest and friend of our family, Fr. Frankhauser would come and stay at the farm and say mass for us. One of us kids would usually get summoned to do a reading or a prayer.

Posing around the old 1936 Buick

The Burns Family 2011

Mom and Dad at Reunion

Mass at the farm 1986
25th Anniversary

Corn shucking contest

Getting ready for the hayride

Cousins

The cousin gals 2014

Cousins 2011

The Burns Extended Family 2011

Coming Home

We deeply missed our old farm on Middleville Road, but we felt fortunate that Mom and Dad were able to continue farming on Cole Road. Every visit home has kept a bit of that farm girl alive within us. Over the years the property has grown to mean more and more to us and has connected us to our roots. One of our favorite places is the front porch in the summer, where we sit and chat and take in the peace of the surroundings. Watching the sun set behind the windmills has become a cherished ritual. Each year we make sure to return during corn season, the second week of August, which we always reserve for this. Being out in the fields, smelling the hay, and eating fresh corn brings us back to our childhood, and we wouldn't trade that feeling for the world.

Teresa with the horses

Sharon with Star

Sharon with horses

Teresa cleaning saddle

4-Wheeler ride to the windmills

Catching the sunset

*Around the firepit at
end of day 2020*

Sharon and Teresa riding horses

Teresa picking grasses

Cooking the turkey outside, Nov. 2022

Our families on sunset ride-Aug. 2022

Teresa on tractor with Dooley

Farmers Daughter's Daughters

When we had daughters of our own, we felt it was important for them to experience a bit of farm life as well. They grew up riding on the tractor with Grandpa and learned how to pick and shuck the perfect ear of corn. They helped decorate the Burns Sweet Corn floats for the Little Falls Canal Days Parades, tossing candy or ears of corn to the crowd. They loved riding through the fields on the three-wheelers and watching the sunset behind the windmills, a tradition they still enjoy today. Over time, they came to appreciate how beautiful and special this place is, just like we do, and why it holds such a deep meaning for us.

The "Pink Lady Club"

Sarah and Megan in field

Maggie bagging corn with Grandpa and Grandma

Sarah with Grandpa 2009

Teresa and Maggie

Maggie on tractor with Grandpa

Megan & Sarah in pumpkin patch

Megan & Sarah riding 3-wheeler with Dad

Megan and Sarah with Grandpa on tractor

Sarah helping Grandpa

Sarah, Megan & Maggie in haymow

Our Float for the Canal Days parade 2015

Maggie and Sarah picking corn 2017

At the Canal Days Parade 2019

At the Canal Days Parade 2022

Sarah and Maggie with Patrick

Megan riding 3-wheeler into the sunset

Megan, Sarah and Maggie

Sharon with daughters 2016

Teresa and her daughter 2017

Life Lessons

Growing up on the farm taught us so many valuable life lessons. We worked for everything we had and we understood the value of a strong work ethic. We learned where our food came from and what it took to produce it. We learned the importance of taking care of the land so it is protected for future generations. We learned that saving money to buy something special was more gratifying than having everything handed to you. We understood the importance of family and helping each other. We respected and loved our animals and felt the pain of losing them. We knew how to read the skies, watch the weather and appreciate its power. We learned that it's important to get to know older folks; they are wiser and can teach you a lot about life. We learned that being a homemaker and a mother is the hardest and most rewarding job there is. We learned to rise to the occasion, always take the high road and to be humble and kind. And we learned that ultimately, despite our wants or efforts, God is the One in charge.

Today's Farms

In recent years, there has been a hopeful shift toward organic and locally grown produce, which has allowed small farms to make a comeback. To help sustain this movement, consider supporting family-owned farms by shopping at local farmer's markets and small produce stands. And if you ever find yourself near exit 29A, off the New York State Thruway, stop and visit Burnsy and Jansy and pick up some sweet corn; you'll be glad you did.

"It isn't the farm who makes the farmer,
it's the love, the hard work and the character." - Unknown

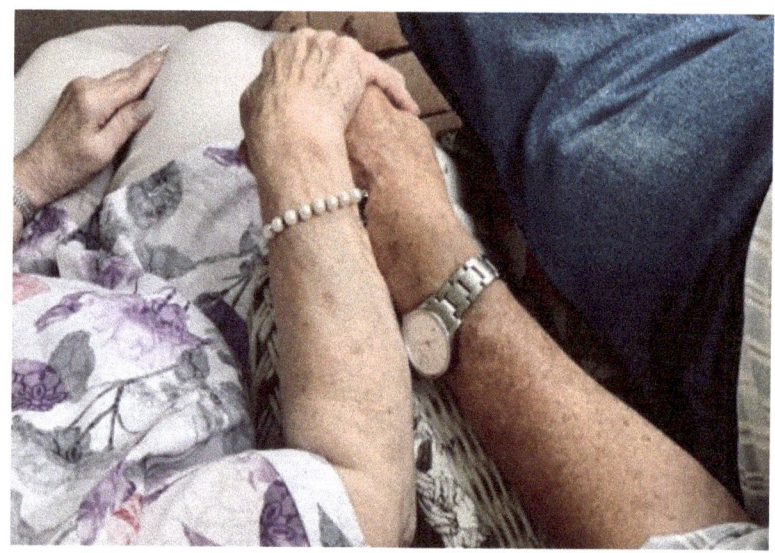

Mom & Dad - 60th Anniversary

About the Authors

Sharon, Patrick, Sarah & Megan

Sharon Burns Ward is a portrait photographer and the owner of Sharon Ward Photography, based in New Hampshire. She has an appreciation for natural light and storytelling through images, and has especially enjoyed documenting farm life over the years. Sharon enjoys spending time at the lake, going for walks, and relaxing with family and friends. She resides in Nashua, NH with her husband Patrick, and their Golden Retriever, Bodie. Their two daughters, Megan and Sarah, also reside in New Hampshire.

Teresa Burns Callahan is a Physician Assistant in Family Medicine. She enjoys a good cup of tea and working in her garden. Teresa lives in Newington, NH with her husband Martin, daughter Maggie and their pets—a Shetland Sheepdog, Maisy, a Maine Coon, Willow and short hair tuxedo, Tilly.

Teresa, Martin & Maggie

www.ingramcontent.com/pod-product-compliance
Lightning Source LLC
Chambersburg PA
CBHW041116120626
46547CB00019B/2736